Voltaire
1694–1778

PENGUIN BOOKS — GREAT IDEAS

Miracles and Idolatry

Voltaire

Miracles and Idolatry

TRANSLATED BY
THEODORE BESTERMAN

PENGUIN BOOKS — GREAT IDEAS

PENGUIN BOOKS

Published by the Penguin Group
Penguin Books Ltd, 80 Strand, London WC2R ORL, England
Penguin Group (USA) Inc., 375 Hudson Street, New York, New York 10014, USA
Penguin Group (Canada), 10 Alcorn Avenue, Toronto, Ontario, Canada M4V 3B2
(a division of Pearson Penguin Canada Inc.)
Penguin Ireland, 25 St Stephen's Green, Dublin 2, Ireland
(a division of Penguin Books Ltd)
Penguin Group (Australia), 250 Camberwell Road,
Camberwell, Victoria 3124, Australia (a division of Pearson Australia Group Pty Ltd)
Penguin Books India Pvt Ltd, 11 Community Centre,
Panchsheel Park, New Delhi – 110 017, India
Penguin Group (NZ), cnr Airborne and Rosedale Roads, Albany,
Auckland 1310, New Zealand (a division of Pearson New Zealand Ltd)
Penguin Books (South Africa) (Pty) Ltd, 24 Sturdee Avenue,
Rosebank 2196, South Africa

Penguin Books Ltd, Registered Offices: 80 Strand, London WC2R ORL, England

www.penguin.com

Dictionnaire Philosophique first published 1764
This translation first published in Penguin Classics 1972
This selection published in Penguin Books 2005

4

Translation copyright © Theodore Besterman, 1972

Taken from the Penguin Classics edition of the *Philosophical Dictionary*
translated and edited by Theodore Besterman

Set by Rowland Phototypesetting Ltd, Bury St Edmunds, Suffolk
Printed in England by Clays Ltd, St Ives plc

Contents

Angel

Angel, in Greek, *messenger*; we shall hardly know more of them when we learn that the Persians had *Peris*, the Hebrews *Malakim*, the Greeks their *Daimonoi*.

But what we shall perhaps find more instructive is the fact that one of mankind's first notions has always been to place intermediary beings between divinity and us. It is these demons, these genii that antiquity invented. Princes were seen to intimate their orders through messengers, therefore divinity also sends its couriers: Mercury, Iris were couriers, messengers.

The Hebrews, the only people guided by divinity itself, at first gave no names to the angels god finally deigned to send them. They borrowed the names given to them by the Chaldeans when the Jewish nation was captive in Babylonia, Michael and Gabriel were first named by Daniel, a slave of that people. The Jew Tobit, who lived at Nineveh, knew the angel Raphael, who travelled with his son to help him collect some money which the Jew Gabael owed him.

In the laws of the Jews, that is, *Leviticus* and *Deuteronomy*, there is not the slightest reference to the existence of angels, let alone their worship. Moreover, the Sadducees did not believe in angels.

But they are talked about a great deal in the histories of the Jews. The angels were corporeal. They had wings on their backs, as the Gentiles pretended that Mercury had on his heels. Sometimes they hid their wings under their clothes. How could they have lacked bodies since they drank and ate, and the inhabitants of Sodom wanted to commit the sin of paederasty with the angels who visted Loth?

The ancient Jewish tradition, according to Maimonides, acknowledges ten degrees, ten orders of angels: 1. The *chaios acodesh*, pure, saintly. 2. The *ofamin*, swift. 3. The *oralim*, the strong. 4. The *chasmalim*, the flames. 5. The *seraphim*, sparks. 6. The *malachim*, angels, messengers, deputies. 7. The *eloim*, the gods or judges. 8. The *ben eloim*, children of the gods. 9. *cherubim*, images. 10. *ychim*, the animated.

The story of the fall of the angels is not in the books of Moses; the first reported witness to it is that of the prophet Isaiah, who, apostrophizing the king of Babylon, exclaimed: 'What has become of the extorter of tribute? The pines and the cedars rejoice in his fall; how are you fallen from heaven, oh Hellel, star of the morning?' This Hellel has been translated by the Latin word *Lucifer*; then the name of Lucifer was given allegorically to the prince of the angels who battled in heaven; and finally this name, which means phosphorus and dawn, has become the name of the devil.

The Christian religion is based on the fall of the angels. Those who rebelled were thrown down from the spheres they inhabited into the hell at the centre of the earth, and became devils. A devil in the shape of a serpent tempted Eve, and damned mankind. Jesus came to redeem mankind and to triumph over the devil, who still tempts us. Nevertheless this fundamental tradition is found only in the apocryphal book of *Enoch*, and even there in a form quite different from the accepted tradition.

In his 109th letter saint Augustine does not hesitate to endow both good and evil angels with slender and agile bodies. Pope Gregory II reduced to nine choirs, nine hierarchies or orders, the ten choirs of angels recognized by the Jews: they are the seraphim, cherubim, thrones, dominations, virtues, powers, archangels and finally the angels who give that name to eight other hierarchies.

In their temple the Jews had two cherubim, each with two heads, one of an ox and the other of an eagle, with six wings. Today we paint them in the image of a flying head, with two little wings below the ears. We paint the angels and archangels in the image of youth, with two wings on their backs. As for the thrones and dominations, nobody has yet taken it into his head to paint them.

Saint Thomas, in the second article of question 108, says that the thrones are as close to god as the cherubim and seraphim because it is on them that god is seated. Scotus has counted a thousand million angels. The ancient mythology of the good and evil genii having passed from the east to Greece and to Rome we hallow this view in accepting that every man has a good and an evil angel, one of whom helps and the other harms him from his birth until his death; but we do not yet know whether these good and evil angels pass continuously from one post to another, or whether they are relieved by others. On this matter consult the *Summa* of saint Thomas.

It is not precisely known where the angels live, whether it is in the air, in the void, or the planets: god has not wished us to know it.

Animals

What a pitiful thing, what poor stuff it is to say that animals are machines deprived of knowledge and feeling, which always perform their operations in the same way, which learn nothing, which improve nothing, etc.!

What! this bird which makes its nest semi-circular when it is attached to a wall, which builds it in a quarter-circle when it is in a corner, and makes it circular in a tree, this bird does everything in the same way? This gun dog you have trained for three months: does he not know more at the end of that time than he knew before your lessons? Does the canary immediately repeat the tune you are teaching him? Do you not spend much time in teaching him? Have you not seen that it makes mistakes and corrects itself?

Do you judge that I have feelings, memory, ideas because I speak to you? Well! I do not speak to you; you see me come home looking distressed, search anxiously for a paper, open the desk in which I remember having put it, find it, read it with joy. You judge that I have experienced the feeling of distress and that of pleasure, that I have memory and knowledge.

Judge in the same way this dog who has lost his master, who has searched for him with mournful cries in every path, who comes home agitated, restless, who runs up and down the stairs, who goes from room to room, who at last finds his beloved master in his study, and shows him his joy by the tenderness of his cries, by his leaps, by his caresses.

Barbarians seize this dog who so prodigiously surpasses man in friendship. They nail him to a table and dissect him alive to show you the mesenteric veins. You discover in him all the same organs of feeling that you possess. Answer me, mechanist, has nature arranged all the springs of feeling in this animal in order that he should not feel? Does he have nerves to be impassive? Do not assume that nature presents this impertinent contradiction.

But the leaders of this school inquire about the souls of animals. I do not understand this question: A tree has the faculty of receiving in its fibres the sap that circulates in it, of putting forth the buds of its leaves and of its fruit; will you ask me what is the soul of this tree? It has received these endowments; the animal has received those of feeling, of memory, of a certain number of ideas. Who has created all these endowments? Who has given all these faculties? He who has made the grass of the fields to grow, and who makes the earth gravitate towards the sun.

'The souls of animals are substantial forms,' said Aristotle; and after Aristotle the Arab school, and after the Arab school the angelic school, and after the angelic school the Sorbonne, and after the Sorbonne nobody at all.

'The souls of animals are material,' exclaim other philosophers. Those have had no greater success than the others. They were asked in vain what is a material soul; they had to agree that it is feeling matter: but what has given it this feeling? It is a material soul, that is, matter has given feeling to matter; they cannot break this circle.

Listen to other animals reasoning about animals. They allege that the soul is a spiritual being which dies with the body: but what proof have you of such a soul? What conception have you of this spiritual being which in reality has feeling, memory and its part of ideas and arrangements, but which will never know what a child of six knows? On what ground do you imagine that this being, which is not body, dies with the body? The greatest donkeys are those who have alleged that this soul is neither body nor spirit. There's a fine system! By spirit we can only understand something unknown which is not body: hence the system of these gentlemen comes down to this, that the soul of an animal is a substance which is neither body nor something which is not body.

What can be the cause of so many contradictory errors? It is the habit men have always had of examining what a thing is before knowing whether it exists. The mobile tongue, the valve of a bellows, is called the soul of the bellows. What is this soul? It is a name I have given to this valve which descends, lets the air in, raises itself, and pushes it through a tube when I agitate the bellows.

Here we have no soul distinct from the machine. But what operates the animals' bellows? I have already told you; he who operates the stars. The philosopher who said, '*Deus est anima brutorum*' [God is the soul of animals], was right; but he should have gone further.

Anti-trinitarians

There are heretics who might not be regarded as Christians. Nevertheless they recognize Jesus to be saviour and mediator; but they dare to maintain that nothing is more contrary to strict reason than what is taught among Christians about the trinity of persons in a single divine essence, the second of which was begotten by the first, and the third of which proceeds from the two others.

That this unintelligible doctrine is nowhere found in scripture.

That no passage can be produced that authorizes it and to which, without in any way departing from the spirit of the text, a clearer, more natural meaning cannot be given, one more consistent with common sense and the basic and immutable truths.

That to maintain, as do their adversaries, that there are several distinct *persons* in the divine essence, and that it is not the eternal who is the only true god, but that the son and the holy ghost must be added to them, is to introduce the crudest and most dangerous error into the church of Jesus Christ, since it manifestly encourages polytheism.

That it implies a contradiction to say that there is only one god and that nevertheless there are three *persons*, each of which is truly god.

That this distinction, one essence and three persons, was never in scripture.

That it is obviously false, since it is certain that there are no fewer *essences* than *persons*, nor *persons* than *essences*.

That the three persons of the trinity are either three different substances, or accidents of the divine essence, or that same essence without distinction.

That in the first case three gods are created.

That in the second case god is composed of accidents and one worships accidents and metamorphoses accidents into persons.

That in the third case an indivisible subject is uselessly and groundlessly divided, and what is not distinguished in itself is distinguished into *three*.

That if it is said that the three *personalities* are neither different substances in the divine essence, nor accidents of that essence, one would have to be at some pains to convince oneself that they are anything.

That it must not be believed that the most rigid and the most convinced *trinitarians* themselves have any clear idea of the manner in which the three *hypostases* subsist in god without dividing his substance and consequently without multiplying it.

That saint Augustine himself, after he had advanced a thousand reasonings as false as they are obscure on this subject, was obliged to admit that nothing intelligible could be said about it.

Then they quote this father's words, which are in fact very singular: 'When it is asked', says he, 'what are the *three*, human language is found inadequate, and there are no terms to express them: yet it is said that there are *three persons*, not in order to say something, but because we must speak and not remain silent. *Dictum est tres personae, non ut aliquid diceretur, sed ne taceretur'* (*De Trinitate* V.ix).

That the modern theologians have not elucidated this matter any better.

That when they are asked what they understand by this word *person*, they explain it only by saying that it is a certain incomprehensible distinction that causes one to distinguish in a numerically single nature a father, a son and a holy ghost.

That the explanation they give of the terms *to beget* and *to proceed* is not more satisfactory since it comes down to saying that these terms indicate certain incomprehensible relationships between the three persons of the trinity.

That from all this we can gather that the basic argument between them and the orthodox turns on the question whether there are in god three distinctions of which we have no notion and between which there are certain relationships of which we do not have any notion either.

From all this they conclude that it would be wiser to abide by the authority of the apostles, who never spoke of the trinity, and to banish from religion for ever all terms which are not in the scriptures, such as *trinity, person, essence, hypostasis, hypostatic and personal union, incarnation, generation, procession*, and so many more like them, which, being absolutely meaningless, since they have no real representative being in nature, can provoke only false, vague, obscure and incomplete ideas in the understanding.

Let us add to this article what dom Calmet says in his dissertation on this passage from the epistle of *John* the evangelist: 'There are three who bear witness on earth, the spirit, and the water, and the blood: and the three agree in one. There are three who bear witness in heaven, the Father, the Word, and the Spirit; and these three are one.' Dom Calmet admits that these two passages are not in any ancient *Bible*; and it would indeed have been strange if saint John had spoken of the trinity in a letter, without saying a single word about it in his gospel. No trace of this dogma is to be found in the canonical gospels, nor in the apocryphal ones. All these reasons could excuse the anti-trinitarians had the councils not taken their decisions. But as heretics make light of councils, we are at a loss to know how to confound them. Let us simply believe and hope that they believe.

Apocalypse

Justin Martyr, who wrote about the year 170 of our era, was the first who mentioned the *Apocalypse* [book of *Revelation*]; he attributed it to the apostle John the evangelist. In his dialogue with Trypho, this Jew asks Justin whether he does not believe that Jerusalem would be restored one day. Justin replies that like all right-thinking Christians he thinks it will. 'There was among us', he says, 'a certain personage named John, one of the twelve apostles of Jesus; he predicted that the faithful would pass a thousand years in Jerusalem.'

This reign of a thousand years was an opinion long held by Christians. It was a period much favoured among the gentiles. The souls of the Egyptians recovered their bodies at the end of a thousand years. In Virgil souls in purgatory were tried during the same space of time, *et mille per annos* [and for a thousand years]. The new Jerusalem of a thousand years was to have twelve doors in memory of the twelve apostles; its form was to be square; its length, width and height were to be 12,000 *stadia*, that is, 500 leagues, so that the houses were also to be 500 leagues high. It would have been rather disagreeable to live on the top floor; still, this is what the *Apocalypse* says in Chapter XXI.

Justin is the first who attributed the *Apocalypse* to saint John, but some people have challenged his testimony because in this same dialogue with the Jew Trypho he says that according to the narrative of the apostles when Jesus Christ went into the Jordan he made the waters of this river boil, and set them on fire, though this is not found in any of the apostles' writings.

The same saint Justin confidently cites the oracles of the sybils. What is more, he claims to have seen in the Egyptian Pharos the remains of the madhouses in which the seventy-two interpreters were confined in Herod's time. The testimony of a man who had the misfortune to see these madhouses seems to indicate that the author should have been locked up in them.

Saint Irenaeus, who came later, and who believed also in the millennium, says that he learned from an old man that saint John had written the *Apocalypse*. But saint Irenaeus has been reproached for having written that there must be only four gospels because there are only four parts of the world and four cardinal winds, and because Ezekiel saw only four animals. He calls this reasoning a demonstration. It must be admitted that Irenaeus certainly demonstrated as well as Justin saw.

In his *Electa* Clement of Alexandria mentions only an *Apocalypse* by saint Peter, to which great importance was attached. Tertullian, a great partisan of the millennium, not only asserts that saint John predicted this resurrection and this reign of a thousand years in the city of Jerusalem, but he also claims that this Jerusalem was already beginning to form in the air; all the Christians of Palestine, and even the pagans, had seen it for forty successive days at the end of the night; but unfortunately the city disappeared as soon as the day broke.

In this preface to the gospel of saint John and in his *Homilies* Origen cites the oracles of the *Apocalypse*; but he also cites the oracles of the sybils. Nevertheless saint Denis of Alexandria, who also wrote towards the middle of the third century, says in one of his fragments, conserved by Eusebius, that nearly all the doctors rejected the *Apocalypse* as a book devoid of reason; that this book had not been composed by saint John but by one Cerinthus, who borrowed a great name to give his dreams more weight.

The council of Laodicea, held in 360, did not include the *Apocalypse* among the canonical books. It was very singular that Laodicea, which was a church to which the *Apocalypse* was addressed, rejected a treasure destined for it, and that the bishop of Ephesus, who attended the council, also rejected this book by saint John, who was buried in Ephesus.

It was visible to all eyes that saint John still moved in his grave, and constantly made the earth rise and fall. Nevertheless the same people who were sure that saint John was not really dead were also sure that he had not written the *Apocalypse*. But those who believed in the millennium were unshakable in their opinion. Sulpicius Severus, in his *Sacred history*, book ix, calls insensate and impious those who did not accept the *Apocalypse*. Finally, after much hesitation, after opposition in council after council, the view of Sulpicius Severus prevailed. The matter having been elucidated, the church decided that the *Apocalypse* is incontestably by saint John: so there is no appeal.

Each Christian community has applied to itself the

prophecies contained in this book; the English have found in it the revolutions of Great Britain; the Lutherans the troubles of Germany; the French protestants the reign of Charles IX and the regency of Catherine de Medicis. They are all equally right. Bossuet and Newton both wrote commentaries on the *Apocalypse*; but on the whole the eloquent declamations of the one and the sublime discoveries of the other have done them greater honour than their commentaries.

Atheist, atheism

I

In former times anybody who possessed a secret in one of the crafts ran the risk of being taken for a sorcerer; every new sect was accused of butchering children in its mysteries; and every philosopher who turned aside from the jargon of the schools was accused of atheism by fanatics and rascals, and condemned by fools.

Anaxagoras dared to maintain that the sun is not guided by Apollo riding in a quadriga: and he was called an atheist and obliged to flee.

Aristotle was accused by a priest of atheism; and, not succeeding in having his accuser punished, retired to Chalcas. But what is most odious in the history of Greece is the death of Socrates. Aristophanes (whom the commentators admire because he was a Greek, forgetting that Socrates also was a Greek) was the first who accustomed the Greeks to regard Socrates as an atheist.

This comic poet, who was neither comic nor a poet, would not have been allowed in our society to write farces for the fair of Saint-Laurent: he appears to me to be lower and more contemptible than Plutarch depicts him. This is what the wise Plutarch says of this humbug: 'The language of Aristophanes betrays his wretched character: it consists of the lowest and most disgusting quips; even the people do not find him amusing, and to men of judgement and honour he is insupportable; his arrogance is unbearable and decent people detest his malignity.'

This then is the Tabarin [buffoon] whom, by the way, mme Dacier, the admirer of Socrates, dared to admire: this is the man who from afar prepared the poison with which infamous judges put to death the most virtuous man in Greece.

The tanners, cobblers and dressmakers of Athens applauded a farce in which Socrates was shown hoisted in the air in a basket, announcing that there was no god, and boasting that he had stolen a coat while teaching philosophy. An entire people, whose bad government authorized such infamous liberties, well deserved what happened to it: to become slaves of the Romans and today of the Turks.

Let us pass over the whole period of time between the Roman republic and ourselves. The Romans, much wiser than the Greeks, never persecuted any philosopher for his opinions. This cannot be said of the barbarian peoples which succeeded the Roman empire. As soon as the emperor Frederick II quarrelled with the popes, he was accused of being an atheist and of being the author, with his chancellor de Vineis, of the book of the *Three Impostors*.

When our great chancellor de L'Hospital declared himself against the persecutions, he was at once accused of atheism, *Homo doctus, sed verus atheos*. A Jesuit, as inferior to Aristophanes as Aristophanes is inferior to Homer, a wretch whose name has become ridiculous even among the fanatics, in a word, the Jesuit Garasse, found atheists everywhere: this is what he called all those against whom he burst out. He called Théodore de Bèze an atheist. It was he who misled the public about Vanini.

Vanini's unhappy end does not move us with indignation and pity like that of Socrates because Vanini was only a foreign pedant without merit, but after all Vanini was not an atheist, as has been alleged; he was precisely the opposite. He was a poor Neapolitan priest, a preacher and theologian by trade, a merciless arguer about quiddities and universals, *et utrum chimera bombinans in vacuo possit comedere secundas intentiones*. But for the rest, there was not a drop of atheism in him. His notion of god was theologically most sound and correct. 'God is his principle and his end, father of the one and the other, and needing neither the one nor the other; eternal without being in time, present everywhere without being anywhere. No past or future exists for him, he is everywhere and beyond everything, governing everything, and having everything, immutable, infinite without parts; his power is his will', etc.

Vanini prided himself on reviving Plato's fine conception, embraced by Averroes, that god had created a chain of beings, from the smallest to the greatest, whose last link is attached to his eternal throne: an idea, in truth, more sublime than true, but which is as far removed from atheism as being is from nothingness.

He travelled to make his fortune and to engage in disputations; but unfortunately disputation is the road that leads away from fortune; one makes as many irreconcilable enemies as one finds learned men or pedants with whom to argue. The misfortune of Vanini had no other cause; his heat and rudeness in dispute earned him the hatred of some theologians; and having had a quarrel with one Francon or Franconi, this Francon, the friend of his enemies, of course accused him of being an atheist who taught atheism.

This Francon or Franconi, aided by a few witnesses, had the barbarity to maintain during the trial what he had asserted. When cross-examined about what he thought of the existence of god, Vanini answered that, like the church, he worshipped one god in three persons. Picking up a straw he said: 'This trifle is enough to prove that there is a creator.' Then he pronounced a very fine discourse on vegetation and motion, and on the necessity for a supreme being without whom there would be neither motion nor vegetation.

Grammont, the presiding judge, then at Toulouse, reports this discourse in his *History of France*, today quite forgotten; and this same Grammont, because of an incredible prejudice, alleges that Vanini said all this from 'vanity, or from fear, rather than from an inner conviction'.

On what can the *président* Grammont's rash and atrocious judgement be based? It is obvious that Vanini's answer should have secured his acquittal on the charge of atheism. But what happened? This unhappy foreign priest also dabbled in medicine. They found a big live toad which he kept at home in a vessel full of water, and of course he was accused of being a sorcerer. They alleged that this toad was the god he worshipped. An impious meaning was given to several passages in his books, which is very easy and very commonly done, by taking objections for replies, by interpreting malignantly some ambiguous phrases, by poisoning an innocent expression. The faction that oppressed him finally extorted from the judges the sentence that condemned the unhappy man to death.

To justify this death it was clearly necessary to accuse the wretched man of the most frightful things. The Minim and very minimal Mersenne pushed lunacy so far as to print that Vanini 'left Naples with twelve of his apostles to convert all the nations to atheism'. How pitiful! How could a poor priest have had twelve men in his pay? How could he have persuaded twelve Neapolitans to travel at great expense, at the peril of their lives, to spread everywhere this abominable and revolting doctrine? Would a king be powerful enough to pay twelve preachers of atheism? Nobody before father Mersenne had put forward so enormous an absurdity. But it has been repeated after him, the newspapers, the historical dictionaries have been infected with it; and the world, which loves sensations, has believed this legend without question.

Bayle himself, in his *Pensées diverses*, speaks of Vanini as an atheist; he used this example to support his paradox 'that a society of atheists can exist'. He assures us that Vanini was a very moral man and that he was the martyr of his philosophic views. He is equally mistaken on both these points. The priest Vanini tells us in the *Dialogue* he wrote in imitation of Erasmus that he had had a mistress called Isabella. He was as bold in his writings as in his conduct, but he was not an atheist.

A century after his death the learned La Croze and the writer who took the name of Philète sought to justify him; but as nobody takes any interest in the memory of an unhappy Neapolitan, a very bad author, hardly anybody reads these apologies.

In his *Athei detecti*, the Jesuit Hardouin, more learned than Garasse, accuses Descartes, Arnauld, Pascal, Nicole, Malebranche of atheism: fortunately they did not suffer Vanini's fate.

From all these facts I pass on to the ethical problem debated by Bayle, that is, *whether a society of atheists could exist*. Let us first observe on this point the enormous extent to which men contradict themselves when disputing: those who have argued with the greatest vehemence against Bayle's opinion, those who have denied with the greatest insults the possibility of a society of atheists, have since maintained with the same dauntlessness that atheism is the religion by which China is governed.

They are certainly mistaken about the Chinese government; all they had to do was to read the edicts of the emperors of this vast country, they would have seen that these edicts are sermons, which everywhere speak of a supreme being, ruler, avenger and remunerator.

But at the same time they are no less mistaken about the impossibility of a society of atheists; and I do not know how M. Bayle could have forgotten a striking example which could have made his cause victorious.

In what respect does a society of atheists seem impossible? It is because men who are unchecked are supposed to be incapable of living together; because the law is helpless against secret crimes; because a vengeful god is needed to punish in this world or the next the wicked who have avoided human justice.

It is true that the laws of Moses did not teach a future life, threatened no punishments after death, did not teach the first Jews the immortality of the soul; but the Jews, far from being atheists, far from seeking to avoid divine vengeance, were the most religious of all men. Not only did they believe in the existence of an eternal god, but they believed that he was always present in their midst; they were terrified of being punished in themselves, in their children, in their posterity to the fourth generation, and this check was very powerful.

But among the gentiles several sects had no such check: the sceptics doubted everything; the Academics suspended their judgement on everything; the Epi-cureans were convinced that the divinity could not meddle in human affairs, and at bottom acknowledged no divinity. They were certain that the soul is not a substance but a faculty that is born and perishes with the body; therefore they bore no yoke but that of morality and honour. The Roman senators and knights were true atheists, for the gods did not exist for men who neither feared them nor hoped for anything from them. Thus in Caesar's and Cicero's time the Roman senate was really an assembly of atheists.

In his harangue for Cluentius the great orator said to the assembled senate: 'What harm does death do him? We reject all the inept fables about hell. What then has death taken from him? Nothing but the feeling of pain.'

Caesar, Catalina's friend, wishing to save his friend's life from this same Cicero, did he not object that to put a criminal to death is not to punish him, that death is nothing, that it is only the end of our sufferings, that it is a happy moment rather than a disastrous one? Did not Cicero and the entire senate yield to this reasoning? The conquerors and legislators of the known world were thus clearly a society of men who had no fear of the gods, who were true atheists.

Bayle next inquires whether idolatry is more dangerous than atheism, whether it is a greater crime not to believe in the divinity than to have unworthy opinions about it. In this he shares the views of Plutarch: he believes that it is better to have no opinion than a bad one. But with all due deference to Plutarch it is obvious that it was infinitely better for the Greeks to fear Ceres, Neptune and Jupiter than to fear nothing at all. It is obvious that the sanctity of oaths is necessary, and that we must have confidence rather in those who think that a false oath will be punished, than in those who think that they can take a false oath with impunity. It is indubitable that it is infinitely more useful in a civilized city to have even a bad religion than none at all.

It would thus appear that Bayle should rather have inquired which is the more dangerous, fanaticism or atheism. Fanaticism is certainly a thousand times more baneful, for atheism does not inspire bloody passions, but fanaticism does; atheism does not discountenance crime, but fanaticism causes crimes to be committed. Let us suppose, with the author of the *Commentarium rerum Gallicarum*, that the chancellor de L'Hospital was an atheist. He enacted only wise laws and counselled only moderation and concord: the fanatics committed the massacres of saint Bartholomew. Hobbes was taken for an atheist. He led a calm and innocent life: the fanatics of his time deluged England, Scotland and Ireland with blood. Spinoza was not only an atheist, but he taught atheism: it was certainly not he who shared the judicial assassination of Barneveldt, it was not he who tore to pieces the two brothers de Witt and ate them on the grill.

For the most part atheists are bold and misguided scholars who reason badly and who, unable to understand the creation, the origin of evil, and other difficulties, have recourse to the hypothesis of the eternity of things and of necessity.

The ambitious, the voluptuous, hardly have the time to reason, and to adopt a bad system; they have other things to do than to compare Lucretius with Socrates. This is the way things are nowadays.

It was not so in the Roman senate, which was almost entirely composed of men who were atheists in both theory and practice, that is, who believed neither in providence nor in the future life. This senate was an assembly of philosophers, voluptuaries and ambitious men, all very dangerous, and who destroyed the republic. Epicureanism persisted under the emperors: the senate's atheists had been sedition-mongers in the times of Sulla and Caesar; under Augustus and Tiberius they were atheist slaves.

I should want no dealings with an atheist prince who thought it useful to have me pounded in a mortar: I am quite sure that I would be pounded. If I were a sovereign I should want no dealings with atheist courtiers whose interest it was to have me poisoned: I should have to take antidotes at random every day. It is thus absolutely necessary for princes and peoples to have deeply engraved in their minds the notion of a supreme being, creator, ruler, remunerator and avenger.

There are atheist peoples, says Bayle in his *Pensées sur les comètes*. The Kaffirs, the Hottentots, the Topinamboos, and many other small nations have no god. That may be so, but it does not mean that they deny god. They neither deny nor affirm him: they have never heard of him. Tell them that there is one, and they will readily believe it. Tell them that everything happens in the nature of things, they also believe you. To allege that they are atheists is as relevant as to say that they are anti-Cartesians: they are neither for nor against Descartes. They are real children; a child is neither atheist nor theist, he is nothing.

What conclusion can we draw from all this? That atheism is a monstrous evil in those who govern; and also in learned men even if their lives are innocent, because from their studies they can affect those who hold office; and that, even if not as baleful as fanaticism, it is nearly always fatal to virtue. Above all, let me add that there are fewer atheists today than there have ever been, since philosophers have perceived that there is no vegetative being without germ, no germ without design, etc., and that grain is not produced by putrefaction.

Unphilosophical mathematicians have rejected final causes, but true philosophers accept them; and as a well-known author has said, a catechist announces god to children, and Newton demonstrates him to wise men.

II

If there are atheists, who is to be blamed if not the mercenary tyrants of souls who, in revolting us against their swindles, compel some feeble spirits to deny the god whom these monsters dishonour? How often have the people's leeches driven prostrated citizens to revolt against the king?

Men fattened on our substance cry out to us: 'Be sure that a she-ass spoke; believe that a fish swallowed up a man and threw him on the shore three days later safe and sound; don't doubt that the god of the universe ordered one Jewish prophet to eat shit (Ezekiel), and another prophet to buy two whores and to beget sons of whores on them (Hosea). These are the very words a god of truth and purity is made to pronounce. Believe a hundred things either obviously abominable or mathematically impossible: otherwise the god of mercy will burn you in the fires of hell, not only for millions of billions of centuries, but throughout all eternity, whether you have a body or whether you have no body.'

These inconceivable stupidities revolt feeble and reckless minds, as well as firm and wise minds. They say: 'Our masters depict god for us as the most senseless and the most barbarous of all kinds, therefore there is no god'; but they ought to say: 'Therefore our masters attribute to god their own absurdities and rages, therefore god is the opposite of what they proclaim, therefore god is as wise and as good as they allege him to be mad and wicked.' This is what wise men conclude. But if a fanatic hears them, he denounces them to a magistrate subservient to the priests; and this magistrate has them burnt on a slow fire, believing that he is avenging and imitating the divine majesty he violates.

Baptism

Baptism, Greek word meaning immersion. Men, who are always guided by their senses, easily imagined that what washes the body washes also the soul. There were great tanks for the priests and the initiates in the vaults under the Egyptian temples. From time immemorial the Indians have purified themselves in the water of the Ganges, and this ceremony is still in great vogue. It passed to the Hebrews: they baptized all the foreigners who embraced the Judaic law, and who would not submit to circumcision; above all the women, who were not made to undergo this operation except in Ethiopia, were baptized; it was a regeneration, which gave a new soul, as in Egypt. See, on this, Epiphanius, Maimonides and the *Gemara*.

John baptized in the Jordan, and he even baptized Jesus, who, however, never baptized anyone, but who deigned to hallow this ancient ceremony. Every symbol is meaningless in itself, and god attaches his grace to the symbol he is pleased to choose. Baptism soon became the chief rite and the seal of the Christian religion. Nevertheless the first fifteen bishops of Jerusalem were all circumcised; it is not certain that they were baptized.

This sacrament was misused in the first centuries of Christianity; nothing was so common as to await the final agony in order to receive baptism. The example of the emperor Constantine is pretty good proof of that. This is how he reasoned: baptism purifies everything; I can therefore kill my wife, my son and all my relations; after which I shall have myself baptized and I shall go to heaven; and in fact that is just what he did. This was a dangerous example; little by little disappeared the custom of waiting for death before taking the plunge into the sacred bath.

The Greeks always conserved baptism by immersion. The Latins, having extended their religion into Gaul and Germany towards the end of the eighth century, and seeing that immersion could kill children in cold countries, substituted simple aspersion, for which they were often anathemized by the Greek church.

Saint Cyprian, bishop of Carthage, was asked if those who had simply had their whole bodies sprinkled were really baptized. He answered in his seventy-sixth letter that 'several churches do not believe that these sprinkled people are Christians; that as for himself he thinks that they are Christians, but that they have infinite less grace than those who have been immersed three times according to custom'.

With the Christians a man was initiated as soon as he was immersed; before this was done he was merely a catechumen. To be initiated it was necessary to have guarantors, sureties, who were given a name corresponding to *godfathers*, so that the church could be sure that the new Christians would be faithful and would not divulge the mysteries. This is why in the first centuries the gentiles were usually as ill-instructed about the mysteries of the Christians as these were about the mysteries of Isis and Eleusis.

Cyril of Alexandria, in his tract against the emperor Julian, expresses himself thus: 'I would speak of baptism were I not afraid that my discourse might reach those who are not initiated.'

As early as the second century they began to baptize children; it was natural that the Christians should want their children to be provided with this sacrament, since they would have been damned without it. It was finally decided that it must be administered to them after a week because among the Jews this was the age at which they were circumcised. This is still the custom in the Greek church. Nevertheless in the third century the practice prevailed of being baptized only at death.

Those who died in the first week were damned, according to the strictest fathers of the church. But Peter Chrysologos, in the fifth century, invented limbo, a kind of mitigated hell, or, precisely, brink of hell, suburb of hell, where go little children who die without baptism, and where resided the patriarchs before the descent of Jesus Christ into hell; so that the view that Jesus Christ descended to limbo and not into hell has prevailed since then.

It has been debated whether a Christian born in the deserts of Arabia could be baptized with sand: the reply was he could not; whether it was permitted to baptize with rose water: and it was decided that pure water was necessary, but that muddy water could be used. It is obvious that all the regulations depended on the prudence of the first pastors who established them.

[. . .]

Baptism: An Addition

What a strange idea, inspired by the wash-pot, that a jug of water washes away all crimes! Now that all children are baptized because a no less absurd idea assumes them all to be criminals, they are all saved until they reach the age of reason and can become guilty. So butcher them as quickly as possible to assure them paradise. This conclusion is so logical that there existed a devout sect who went about poisoning or killing all newly baptized infants. These devotees reasoned perfectly. They said: 'We are doing these little innocents the greatest possible kindness; we are preventing them from being wicked and unhappy in this life, and we are giving them eternal life.'

Cannibals

I have spoken of love. It is hard to pass from people who embrace each other to people who eat each other. It is only too true that there have been cannibals. Some have been found in America. There may still be some, and the cyclops were not the only ones in antiquity who sometimes fed on human flesh. Juvenal reports that among the Egyptians, so wise a people, so famous for its laws, so pious a people, who worshipped crocodiles and onions, the Denderites ate one of their enemy who had fallen into their hands. He does not tell this story on hearsay: this crime was committed almost under his eyes; he was then in Egypt, not far from Dendera. In this connection he cites the Gascons and the Sagantines, who formerly fed on the flesh of their countrymen.

In 1725 four savages were brought from the Mississippi to Fontainebleau. I had the honour to converse with them. Among them was a lady of that country whom I asked whether she had eaten men. She replied very innocently that she had. I appeared a little scandalized. She excused herself by saying that it was better to eat one's dead enemy than to let him be devoured by beasts, and the victors deserved to have the preference. We kill our neighbours in pitched or unpitched battle, and for the meanest rewards prepare meals for the crows and the worms. There is the horror, there is the crime. When one has been killed what does it matter whether one is eaten by a soldier or by a crow or a dog?

We respect the dead more than the living. We ought to respect both. Nations called civilized are right not to put their vanquished enemies on the spit, for if we were permitted to eat our neighbours we would soon eat our fellow countrymen, which would be a mixed blessing for the social virtues. But the civilized nations have not always been civilized; all were for long savage; and in the infinite number of revolutions this globe has undergone, the human species has sometimes been numerous, sometimes very rare. What is happening today to elephants, lions, tigers, whose numbers have much decreased, once happened to mankind. In times when a region was little inhabited by men, they had few arts, they were hunters. The habit of feeding on what they had killed readily caused them to treat their enemies like their stags and their boars. It was superstition that caused human victims to be immolated, it was necessity that caused them to be eaten.

Which is the greater crime, piously to assemble to plunge a knife into the heart of a young girl adorned with fillets, in honour of the divinity, or to eat a villain who has been killed in self-defence?

Nevertheless we have many more examples of girls and boys who have been sacrificed than of girls and boys who have been eaten. The Jews immolated them. This was called the anathema. It was a real sacrifice, and it is commanded in the twenty-seventh chapter of *Leviticus* not to spare the living souls who had been devoted to god, but it is nowhere prescribed that they should be eaten, they are merely threatened with this fate. And Moses, as we have seen, said to the Jews that, if they did not observe these ceremonies, not only would they have the itch but mothers would eat their children. It is true that in Ezekiel's time the Jews must have been in the habit of eating human flesh, for in chapter xxxix he predicts to them that god would make them eat not only the horses of their enemies but also the horsemen and the other warriors. This is definite. And in fact why should the Jews not have been cannibals? It would have been the only thing the people of god lacked to be the most abominable on earth.

I have read in some anecdotes on the history of England in Cromwell's time that a tallow-chandler in Dublin sold excellent candles made of the fat of Englishmen. Some time after one of her customers complained that her candles were no longer so good. 'Alas,' she said, 'it's because we have been short of Englishmen this month.' I ask who were the guiltier, those who murdered Englishmen or this woman who made their grease into candles?

Certain, certainty

'How old is your friend Christopher?'

'Twenty-eight. I have seen his marriage contract and his baptismal certificate. I have known him since his childhood. He is twenty-eight; it is a certainty, I'm certain of it.'

Hardly had I heard the reply of this man, so sure of what he says, and of twenty others who confirmed the same thing, than I discovered that Christopher's baptismal certificate had been antedated by a strange trick for hidden reasons. Those to whom I spoke don't yet know about it. In the meanwhile they're still certain of something false.

If you had asked the entire world before the era of Copernicus: 'Did the sun rise today? did it set?' everybody would have answered you: 'We're absolutely certain of it.' They were certain, and they were mistaken.

Spells, divination, possession were for long the surest things in the world in the eyes of all peoples. What an innumerable crowd of people saw all these fine things and were certain of them! Today this certainty has somewhat diminished.

A young man who was beginning to study geometry called on me. He had not got beyond the definition of triangles. 'Aren't you certain,' I said, 'that the three angles of a triangle are equal to two right angles?' He replied that not only was he not at all certain of it, but that he did not even have a clear idea of this proposition. I demonstrated it to him; he then became very certain of it, and will be so all his life.

That certitude is very different from the others: they were no more than probabilities, and these probabilities, once examined, became errors; but mathematical certitude is immutable and eternal.

I exist, I think, I feel pain. Is all this as certain as a geometric truth? Yes. Why? It is because these truths are proved by the same principle that a thing cannot be and not be at the same time. I cannot at the same time exist and not exist, feel and not feel. A triangle cannot at the same time have and not have 180 degrees, which is the sum of two right angles.

The physical certainty of my existence and of my feelings, and mathematical certainty thus have the same value, although they are of a different kind.

This does not apply to the certainty based on appearances or to the unanimous reports made by men.

'But really!' you tell me, 'aren't you certain that Peking exists? Haven't we got fabrics from Peking? People from different countries, of different opinions, who wrote violently against each other while all preached the truth in Peking, haven't they assured you of the existence of this city?' I answered that it seems to me extremely probable that there was then a city of Peking; but I would not wish to bet my life that this city exists, and I would bet my life at any time that the three angles of a triangle are equal to two right angles.

Something very droll has been published in the *Dic-*

tionnaire encyclopédique. It is maintained there that if all Paris told one that marshal de Saxe had been resurrected, one should be as sure, as certain of it as one would be if told by all Paris that marshal de Saxe had won the battle of Fontenoy. Consider, I beg, how admirable is this reasoning: 'I believe all Paris when they tell me something possible in principle; therefore I must believe all Paris when they tell me something impossible in principle and physically.'

Apparently the author of this article wanted to have a good laugh, and the other author, who goes into raptures at the end of this article and writes against himself, also wanted to have a good laugh. As for me, who have undertaken this little *Dictionary* in order to put questions, I am far from being certain.

Character

From the Greek word *impression, engraving*. It is what nature has engraved in us. Can we efface it? Vast question. If I have a hooked nose and two cat's eyes I can hide them with a mask. Can I do better with the character nature has given me? A man born violent, choleric, presented himself before François I, king of France, to complain of an injustice. The prince's countenance, the respectful conduct of the courtiers, the very place in which he found himself, made a powerful impression on this man; he unconsciously lowered his eyes, his rough voice softened, he presented his request humbly. One would believe him to be naturally as gentle as are (at least at this moment) the courtiers in whose midst he is even disconcerted; but if François I is good at reading faces he will easily realize in his eyes, lowered but alight with hidden fire, in the taut muscles of his face, in his lips pressed against each other, that this man is not so gentle as he is obliged to appear. This man followed him to Pavia, was captured with him, and taken to prison in Madrid with him; the majesty of François I no longer made the same impression on him; he became familiar with the object of his respect. One day, while pulling off the king's riding boots, and pulling them badly, the king, soured by his misfortune, became angry: my man sent the king to the devil, and threw his boots out of the window.

Sixtus V was by nature petulant, obstinate, haughty, impetuous, vindictive, arrogant: his character appears to have been softened by the ordeal of his novitiate. As he began to enjoy some reputation in his order, he lost his temper with an attendant and felled him with his fist. When inquisitor in Venice he exercised his office with insolence. Become cardinal he was possessed *della rabbia papale* [by the furious ambition to become pope]. This rage subdued his nature; he buried his person and his character in obscurity; he shammed humility and ill-health; he was elected pope: in this instant was restored all the elasticity so long restrained by policy; he was the proudest and most despotic of sovereigns.

> *Naturam expellas furca, tamen ipsa redibit.*
> [Nature will always return even if you expel her
> with a pitchfork]
> *Chassez le naturel, il revient au galop.*

Religion, morality put a curb on the power of nature; they cannot destroy it. The drunkard in a cloister, reduced to one glass of cider with each meal, will no longer get drunk, but he will always love wine.

Age weakens the character; it is a tree that produces nothing but a few degenerate fruits, but they are still of the same kind; it gets to be covered with knots and moss, it becomes worm-eaten, but it is still an oak or a pear tree. If we could change our character we would give ourselves one, we would be the masters of nature. Can we give ourselves something? Do we not receive everything? Try to arouse continuous activity in an indolent mass, to freeze with apathy the boiling soul of the impetuous, to inspire a taste for music and poetry into one who lacks taste and an ear: you will no more succeed than if you undertook to give sight to one born blind. We perfect, we mitigate, we hide what nature has placed in us; but we place nothing in ourselves.

A farmer was told: 'You have too many fish in this pond, they will not thrive; there are too many animals in your fields, there is not enough grass, they will lose weight.' After this exhortation it so happened that pike ate half my man's carp, and wolves half of his sheep; the rest fattened. Will he congratulate himself on his management? This countryman is you yourself; one of your passions devours the others and you think you have triumphed over yourself. Do we not really all resemble the old general of ninety who, coming across some young officers who were causing a disturbance with some women of the town, said in a temper: 'Gentlemen, is this the example I give you?'

Councils

All councils are undoubtedly infallible: for they are composed of men. It is impossible for passions, intrigues, the lust for dispute, hatred, jealousy, prejudice, ignorance ever to reign in these assemblies.

But why, it will be asked, have so many councils contradicted each other? It is to try our faith. Each was in the right in its turn.

Roman Catholics now believe only in councils approved by the Vatican; and the Greek Catholics believe only in those approved in Constantinople. Protestants deride them both. Thus everybody should be satisfied.

I shall refer here only to the great councils; the small ones are not worth the trouble.

The first one was that of Nicaea. It was assembled in 325 of the common era, after Constantine had written and sent by the hand of Ozius this noble letter to the rather confused clergy of Alexandria: 'You are quarrelling about something very trivial. These subtleties are unworthy of sensible people.' The thing was to determine whether Jesus was created or uncreated. This has nothing to do with morality, which is the essential point. Whether Jesus was in time or before time, we must none the less be good. After many altercations it was finally decided that the son was as old as the father, and consubstantial with the father. This decision is hardly comprehensible, but it is all the more sublime on that account. Seventeen bishops protested against the decree, and an ancient chronicle of Alexandria, preserved at Oxford, says that 2,000 priests also protested; but prelates pay little attention to simple priests, who are usually poor. Be that as it may, there was no question whatever of the trinity in this first council. The formula reads: 'We believe Jesus consubstantial with the father, god of god, light of light, begotten and not made; we also believe in the holy ghost.' The holy ghost, it must be admitted, was treated pretty off-handedly.

It is reported in the supplement of the council of Nicaea that the fathers, being very perplexed to know which were the cryphal or apocryphal books of the Old and New Testaments, put them all pell-mell on an altar, and the books to be rejected fell to the ground. It is a pity that this elegant procedure has not survived.

After the first council of Nicaea, composed of 317 infallible bishops, another was held at Rimini, and this time the number of infallibles was 400, not counting a big detachment of about 200 at Seleucia. These 600 bishops, after four months of quarrels, unanimously deprived Jesus of his consubstantiality. It has since been restored to him, except among the Socinians; so everything is fine.

One of the great councils was that of Ephesus in 431. Nestorius, bishop of Constantinople, great persecutor of heretics, was himself condemned as a heretic for maintaining that in truth Jesus was really god, but that his mother was not absolutely the mother of god, but the mother of Jesus. It was saint Cyril who had Nestorius condemned; but then the partisans of Nestorius had saint Cyril deposed in the same council: which much embarrassed the holy ghost.

Note very carefully here, dear reader, that the gospel has never said a word about the consubstantiality of the word, nor about the honour Mary had had to be the mother of god, nor about the other disputes which have caused infallible councils to be assembled.

Eutyches was a monk who had much abused Nestorius, whose heresy did not fall short of alleging that Jesus was two persons: which is appalling. The better to contradict his adversary the monk asserted that Jesus had only one nature. A certain Flavian, bishop of Constantinople, maintained against him that it was absolutely necessary for Jesus to have had two natures. A numerous council was assembled at Ephesus in 449. This one was conducted with the quarter-staff, like the little council of Cirta in 355, and a certain conference at Carthage. Flavian's nature became black and blue, and two natures were assigned to Jesus. At the council of Chalcedon, in 451, Jesus was reduced to one nature.

I pass over councils held on account of minute details, and come to the sixth general council, of Constantinople, assembled to determine precisely whether Jesus, having only one nature, had two wills. It will be realized how important this is in order to please god.

This council was called by Constantine the bearded, just as all the others had been by the preceding emperors. The legates of the bishop of Rome sat on the left, the patriarchs of Constantinople and Antioch on the right. I do not know whether the Roman toadies claim the left to be the place of honour. Be this as it may, Jesus obtained two wills from this affair.

The Mosaic law had prohibited images. Painters and sculptors had never done very well among the Jews. It does not appear that Jesus ever possessed any pictures, except perhaps that of Mary painted by Luke. At any rate, Jesus Christ nowhere enjoins the worship of images. Nevertheless Christians worshipped them towards the end of the fourth century, when they had familiarized themselves with the fine arts. This error went so far in the eighth century that Constantine Copronymus assembled in Constantinople a council of 320 bishops, which anathemized the worship of images and branded it as idolatry.

The empress Irene, the same who later had her son's eyes torn out, assembled the second council of Nicaea in 787. In this the worship of images was restored. Nowadays it is sought to justify this council by saying that this worship was one of *dulia* [veneration of the saints] and not of *latria* [veneration of god].

However, be it *latria* or *dulia*, in 794 Charlemagne called another council, at Frankfurt, which stigmatized the second of Nicaea as idolatrous. Pope Adrian IV sent two legates to it but did not convoke it.

The first great council called by a pope was the first Lateran, in 1139. About a thousand bishops were there, but almost nothing was accomplished in it, except that those who said that the church was too rich were anathemized.

There was another Lateran council in 1179, held by pope Alexander III, in which the cardinals for the first time took precedence over the bishops. Only matters of discipline were discussed.

Another great council was the Lateran of 1215. In it pope Innocent III stripped the count of Toulouse of all his possessions, by virtue of excommunication. This was the first council in which there was any question of transubstantiation.

In 1245 took place the general council of Lyon, then an imperial city, during which pope Innocent IV excommunicated the emperor Frederick II, and in consequence deposed him, and forbade him fire and water. It was in this council that the cardinals were given red hats to remind them that they must bathe in the blood of the emperor's supporters. This council brought about the destruction of the house of Swabia, and led to thirty years of anarchy in Italy and Germany.

In the general council of 1311 at Vienne, in Dauphiné, was abolished the order of the Templars, whose leading members had been condemned to the most horrible tortures on the most unsubstantiated accusations.

In 1414 was held the great council of Constance, which contented itself with deposing pope John XXIII, convicted of a thousand crimes, and in which John Huss and Jerome of Prague were burned for being obstinate, since obstinacy is a much greater crime than murder, rape, simony and sodomy.

The great council of Basle in 1431 was not recognized in Rome because it deposed pope Eugene IV, who did not consent to be deposed.

The Romans reckon the fifth Lateran council of 1512 as a general council. It was called by pope Julius II against

Louis XII, king of France, but this warrior-pope died, and the council went up in smoke.

Finally we have the great council of Trent, which does not have authority in France in matters of discipline. However, its dogma is unquestionable, since the holy ghost came every week from Rome to Trent in the courier's trunk, according to fra Paolo Sarpi; but fra Paolo Sarpi smelled a little of heresy.

Enthusiasm

This Greek word means *disturbance of the entrails, internal agitation*. Did the Greeks invent this word to express the shocks felt by the nerves, the dilation and tightening of the bowels, the violent contractions of the heart, the precipitate rush of the fiery spirits that mount from the entrails to the brain when one is deeply moved?

Or was the word *enthusiasm*, from disturbance of the entrails, first given to the contractions of that Pythia who, on the tripod at Delphi, received the spirit of Apollo through a part which seems made only to receive bodies?

What do we understand by enthusiasm? What nuances in our sentiments! Approval, sensibility, emotion, distress, shock, passion, frenzy, madness, fury, rage: these are all the states a wretched human soul can pass through.

A geometrician watches a touching tragedy: he sees only that it is well constructed. A young man by his side is moved and sees nothing. A woman weeps. Another young man is so carried away that, unhappily for him, he also decides to write a tragedy: he has caught the disease of enthusiasm.

The centurion or military tribune who looked on war simply as a trade in which a little fortune could be made, went calmly into battle like a thatcher climbing a roof. Caesar wept when he saw the statue of Alexander.

Ovid always spoke amusingly about love. Sappho expressed the enthusiasm of this passion; and if it is true that it cost her her life it is because in her case enthusiasm became madness.

The spirit of party marvellously encourages enthusiasm: no faction is without its fanatics.

Enthusiasm is above all the lot of misguided piety. The young fakir who sees the tip of his nose when praying gradually works himself up until he believes that if he loads himself with chains weighing fifty pounds the supreme being will be much obliged to him. He goes to sleep with his imagination filled with Brahma, and inevitably sees him in his dreams. Sometimes sparks even shine from his eyes in the state between sleep and waking: he sees Brahma glittering with light, he has ecstasies, and this disease often becomes incurable.

It is the rarest of things to unite reason with enthusiasm. Reason consists of always seeing things as they are. The drunkard is deprived of his reason when he sees things double. Enthusiasm is precisely like wine: it can excite so much tumult in the blood vessels, and such violent vibrations in the nerves, that the reason is entirely destroyed. It can cause only slight jolts, which merely produce a little more activity in the brain. This is what happens in great outbursts of eloquence, and above all in sublime poetry. Rational enthusiasm is the attribute of great poets. This rational enthusiasm is the perfection of their art. In other times it led to the belief that they were inspired by the gods, a thing that has never been said of the other artists.

How can reason govern enthusiasm? This is because

a poet first sketches the structure of his canvas: the reason then holds the brush. But when he proceeds to animate his personages and to endow them with passions, then the imagination kindles, enthusiasm takes over: it is a race horse carried away headlong, but its course has been properly laid out.

Equality

What does a dog owe to a dog, and a horse to a horse? Nothing, no animal depends on his like; but man having received the ray of divinity called *reason*, what is the result? Slavery throughout almost the whole world.

Were this world what it seems that it should be, that is, if man found everywhere on it easy and assured subsistence and a climate appropriate to his nature, it is clear that it would have been impossible for one man to subjugate another. Let this globe be covered with wholesome fruit; let the air which must contribute to our life no longer give us illness and death; let man require no other lodging and no other bed than those of the deer and the stag: then the Genghis Khans and the Tamerlanes would have no other servants than their children, who would be upright enough to help them in their old age.

In this natural state enjoyed by all quadrupeds, birds and reptiles, man would be as happy as they, domination would then be a chimera, an absurdity which would occur to nobody: for why seek for servitors when you need no service?

If some individual with a tyrannical head and vigorous arm got the idea of subjugating a neighbour less strong than he, the thing would be impossible: the oppressed would be 100 leagues away before the oppressor could take action.

Thus all men would necessarily be equal if they were without needs. The poverty characteristic of our species subordinates one man to another. It is not inequality that is the real evil, but dependence. It matters very little that some man is called his highness, and another his holiness; but it is hard to serve one or the other.

A numerous family has cultivated good land. Two small neighbouring families have barren and obstinate fields. It is obvious enough that the two poor families must serve the opulent family or murder it. One of the two indigent families offers its labour to the rich to get bread; the other attacks it and is beaten. The former family originated servants and labourers, the defeated family slaves.

It is impossible on our wretched globe for men living in society not to be divided into two classes, one of oppressors, the other of the oppressed; and these subdivide into a thousand, and the thousand have further gradations.

All the oppressed are not absolutely unhappy. Most of them are born in that state, and continual work prevents them from feeling their condition too keenly; but when they feel it, then we have wars like that in Rome of the popular party against that of the senate, and those of the peasants in Germany, in England, in France. All these wars end sooner or later by the enslavement of the people because the powerful have the money, and in a state money is the master of everything:

I say in a state, because it is not so in every nation. The nation making the best use of the sword will always subjugate that having more gold and less courage.

Every man is born with a powerful enough desire for domination, wealth and pleasure, and with much taste for idleness. Consequently every man would like to have other people's money and wives or women, to be their master, to subjugate them to all his caprices, and to do nothing, or at least to do only very agreeable things. Obviously, having such amiable dispositions, it is as impossible for men to be equal as it is impossible for two preachers or two professors of theology not to be jealous of one another.

Mankind cannot subsist at all unless there is an infinite number of useful men who possess nothing at all. For a prosperous man will certainly not leave his land to cultivate yours; and if you need a pair of shoes it is not a judge who will make them for you. Equality is thus at once the most natural and the most chimerical of things.

As men are extreme in everything whenever possible, this inequality has been exaggerated. In some countries it has been claimed that a citizen is not entitled to leave the country in which he is born by chance. The meaning of this law is obviously: *This country is so bad and so badly governed that we forbid every individual to leave it, for fear that everybody leave it.* Do better: make all your subjects wish to remain at home and strangers to come to you.

Every man has the right to believe himself, at the bottom of his heart, entirely equal to all other men. It does not follow from this that a cardinal's cook should order his master to prepare his dinner; but the cook can say: 'I'm a man like my master, like him I am born in tears; like me he will die with the same sufferings and the same ceremonies. Both of us perform the same animal functions. If the Turks capture Rome, and I am then a cardinal and my master a cook, I will take him into my service.' All this speech is reasonable and just; but until the Grand Turk captures Rome the cook must do his duty, or every human society is perverted.

As for a man who is neither a cardinal's cook nor endowed with any other public office; as for a private person of modest views, but who is annoyed because he is received everywhere with an air of patronage or disdain, who sees clearly that several monsignors have no more knowledge, no more intelligence, no more virtue than he, and who is sometimes wearied to find himself in their waiting rooms, what should he do? He should leave.

Fatherland

A fatherland is a composite of several families; and as we usually stand by our family out of self-love when we have no conflicting interest, so because of the same self-love we support our town or village, which we call our fatherland. The bigger the fatherland the less we love it, because divided love is weaker. It is impossible to love tenderly too numerous a family which we hardly know.

He who burns with ambition to become aedile, tribune, praetor, consul, dictator, cries out that he loves his country, and he loves only himself. Every man wants to be sure that he can sleep at home without another man arrogating to himself the power to make him sleep elsewhere. Every man wants to be sure of his fortune and his life. Thus, all having the same wishes, it turns out that private interest becomes the general interest: when we express our hopes for ourselves we are expressing them for the republic.

There cannot be a state on earth which was not first governed as a republic: it is the normal course of human nature. A few families first assembled against the bears and the wolves. The family which had grain exchanged it with that which had only wood.

When we discovered America we found all the tribes divided into republics. There were only two kingdoms in all this part of the world. Only two out of 1,000 nations were found to be subjugated.

So it was in the ancient world. All was republican in Europe before the petty kings of Etruria and Rome. Republics are still seen today in Africa. Tripoli, Tunis, Algeria, towards the north, still live as men are said to have lived in the first ages of the world, free, equal among themselves, without masters, without subjects, without money, and almost without needs. The flesh of their sheep feeds them, their skins clothe them, huts of wood and earth are their shelters. They stink worse than any other men, but do not know it. They live and die more calmly than we do.

Eight republics without monarchs remain in our Europe: Venice, Holland, Switzerland, Genoa, Lucca, Ragusa, Geneva and San Marino. Poland, Sweden, England can be regarded as republics under a king; but Poland is the only one that takes the name.

Is it better today for one's country to be a monarchical or a republican state? This question has been debated for 4,000 years. Apply for a solution to the rich, they all prefer an aristocracy. Question the people, they want democracy. Only kings prefer a monarchy. How then is it possible that nearly the whole world is governed by monarchs? Ask the rats who proposed to hang a bell round the cat's neck. But in truth the real reason is, as I have said, that men are very seldom worthy to govern themselves.

It is sad that, to be a good patriot, one is often the enemy of the rest of humanity. The elder Cato, that good citizen, when speaking in the senate, always said:

'Such are my views, and let Carthage be destroyed.' To be a good patriot is to want one's city to be enriched by commerce and powerful in arms. It is obvious that a country cannot gain unless another loses, and that it cannot vanquish without causing unhappiness.

So it is the human condition that to wish for the greatness of one's fatherland is to wish evil to one's neighbours. The citizen of the universe would be the man who wishes his country never to be either greater or smaller, richer or poorer.

Flood

Has there ever been a time when the globe was entirely flooded? This is physically impossible.

It may be that the sea covered all parts of the earth one after the other, but that could have happened only by slow stages in a prodigious multitude of centuries. In a period of 500 years the sea has withdrawn from Aigues-Mortes, from Fréjus, from Ravenna, which were great ports, and has left about two leagues of dry ground. At this rate it is evident that it would take the sea 2,500,000 years to move round our globe. What is very remarkable is that this period is very near that taken by the axis of the earth to right itself and coincide with the equator. This movement, which is very probable, has been suspected for fifty years, and can only be completed in a period of more than 2,300,000 years.

The beds, the layers of shells which have been discovered on all sides, at several leagues from the sea, are incontrovertible proof that it has deposited its maritime products little by little on land that once formed the ocean shore. But that water once covered the entire globe at the same time is a chimera absurd in natural science, demonstrated impossible by the laws of gravitation, by the laws of fluids, by the insufficient quantity of water. I do not claim to undermine in any way the great truth of the universal flood reported in the Pentateuch.

On the contrary, it was a miracle, therefore it must be believed; it was a miracle, therefore it was not performed by physical laws.

Everything is miraculous in the story of the flood. It was a miracle that forty days of rain inundated the four quarters of the earth, and that the water should have risen fifteen cubits above all the highest mountains. It was a miracle that there were cataracts, doors, openings in the sky. It was a miracle that all the animals should have proceeded to the ark from every part of the world. It was a miracle that Noah found enough to feed them for ten months. It was a miracle that all the animals found room in the ark with their provisions. It was a miracle that most of them did not die in the ark. It was a miracle that they found food on leaving the ark. It was also a miracle, but of another kind, that a certain Le Pelletier thought that he had explained naturally how all the animals fitted into the ark and fed themselves.

Now the story of the flood being the most miraculous thing we have ever heard of, it would be senseless to explain it. It is one of the mysteries we believe by faith, and faith consists in believing what the reason does not believe, which is another miracle in itself.

Thus the story of the universal flood is like that of the tower of Babel, Balaam's she-ass, the fall of Jericho by the sound of trumpets, water changed into blood, the passage of the Red Sea, and all the prodigies god deigned to perform for the benefit of his people's elect. These are profundities beyond human comprehension.

Great chain of being

The gradation of beings which ascends from the lightest atom to the supreme being, this ladder of the infinite, strikes one with wonder. But when one looks at it attentively this great phantasm vanishes, as formerly all apparitions fled at the crowing of the cock.

At first the imagination is gratified by the imperceptible passage from brute matter to organized matter, from plants to zoophytes, from these zoophytes to animals, from these to man, from man to spirits, from these spirits, dressed in little aerial bodies, to immaterial substances, and finally a thousand different orders of these substances which ascend from beauty to perfection and finally to god himself. This hierarchy much pleases decent folk, who liken it to the pope and his cardinals followed by the archbishops and the bishops, after whom come rectors, vicars, simple priests, deacons, subdeacons; then appear the monks, and the march-past ends with the capuchins.

But there is a rather greater distance between god and his most perfect creatures than between the holy father and the dean of the sacred college. This dean can become pope, but the most perfect of the spirits created by the supreme being cannot become god: there is infinity between god and him.

Nor does this chain, this alleged gradation exist among

the vegetables and the animals which have been destroyed. There are no longer any murex. The Jews were forbidden to eat the griffin and the ixion. These two species have disappeared from the world, whatever Bochart may say. Where then is the chain?

Even if we had not lost several species, it is obvious that they can be destroyed. The lions, the rhinoceros are getting quite rare.

It is very probable that there have been races of men which are no longer found. But I hope that they have all survived, like the whites, the blacks, the Kaffirs, to whom nature has given a skin apron hanging from the belly half way down the thigh, the Samoyedes, whose wives have one beautifully black breast, etc.

Is there not obviously a gap between monkey and man? Is it not easy to imagine an animal with two feet and no feathers, intelligent without having also the power of speech or our appearance, which we could tame, which would answer our signals and serve us? And between this new species and man, could we not imagine others?

Divine Plato, you place in heaven a succession of celestial substances beyond man. For our part, we believe in a few of these substances, because this is taught by our faith. But you, what reason have you for believing in them? It would seem that you have not spoken to Socrates's demon, and good old Er who resuscitated specially to reveal to you the secrets of the other world, taught you nothing about these substances.

The alleged chain is no less interrupted in the physical universe.

What gradation, if you please, between your planets? The moon is forty times smaller than our globe. When you have travelled from the moon through space you come to Venus: it is about as big as the earth. Thence you go to Mercury, which revolves in an ellipse very different from the circle traversed by Venus. It is twenty-seven times smaller than we are, the sun a million times bigger, Mars five times smaller. This last makes its revolution in two years, his neighbour Jupiter in twelve, Saturn in thirty, even though Saturn, the most distant of all, is not as big as Jupiter. Where is the alleged gradation?

And then how can you expect there to be a chain that links everything in the great empty spaces? If there is one it is certainly that which Newton discovered: this is what makes all the globes of the planetary world gravitate towards one another in this immense void.

O Plato, so much admired, I fear that you have told us nothing but fables, and that you have never uttered anything but sophisms!

O Plato! You have done much more evil than you think. I shall be asked how, but I shall not answer.

Hell

As soon as men lived in society they must have noticed that some guilty men eluded the severity of the laws. They punished public crimes. It was necessary to create a check on secret crimes: only religion could be this check. The Persians, the Chaldeans, the Egyptians, the Greeks invented punishments after life; and the Jews alone among all the ancient peoples known to us approved only temporal punishments. It is ridiculous to believe, or to pretend to believe, on the strength of a few very obscure passages, that hell was recognized by the ancient laws of the Jews, by their *Leviticus*, by their decalogue, when the author of these laws does not say a single word that could have the slightest bearing on punishments in the future life. One would be entitled to say to the compiler of the *Pentateuch*: 'You are an irresponsible man, without probity and reason, very unworthy of the name of legislator that you arrogate. What! you know a dogma so repressive, and so necessary to the people, as that of hell, and you do not explicitly proclaim it? And, though it is accepted by all the nations around you, you are content to allow this dogma to be guessed at by some commentators who are to come 4,000 years after you and will torture some of your words to find in them something you have not said. Either you are an ignoramus, who are not aware that this belief was universal in Egypt, in Chaldea, in Persia; or you are very ill-advised, knowing this dogma, not to have made it the basis of your religion.'

The authors of the Jewish laws might at best reply: 'We admit that we are exceedingly ignorant; that we learned to write very late; that our people was a savage and barbaric horde which, as we have shown, wandered for half a century in uninhabitable deserts; that it finally usurped a small country by the most odious rapine and the most detestable cruelties ever recorded in history. We had no intercourse with civilized nations: how can you expect us (the most earthly of men) to have invented a wholly spiritual system?

'We used the word meaning *soul* only in the sense of *life*. We knew our god and his ministers, his angels, only as corporeal beings: the distinction between soul and body, the notion of a life after death, can be the fruit only of long meditation and a very subtle philosophy. Ask the Hottentots and the Negroes, who inhabit a country a hundred times larger than ours, whether they know about a future life. We thought we had done enough in persuading our people that god punishes evil-doers to the fourth generation, whether by leprosy, sudden death, or the loss of what little property it was possible for them to possess.'

One would reply to this defence: 'You have invented a system the absurdity of which is self-evident; for the malefactor who was in good health and whose family prospered would necessarily laugh at you.'

The apologist of the Judaic law would then answer: 'You are mistaken; for there were a hundred criminals who did not reason at all, for every one who thought clearly. The man who, having committed a crime, felt unpunished in himself and in his son, feared for his grandson. Besides, if he did not have some stinking ulcer today, he would get one in the course of a few years, for we were much subject to them. Every family has misfortunes, and it was easy for us to inoculate the belief that these misfortunes were sent by a divine hand, the avenger of secret offences.'

It would be easy to respond to this answer, and to say: 'Your excuse is worthless, for it happens every day that very decent folk lose their health and their goods; and if there is no family that has escaped misfortune, and if these misfortunes are god's punishments, all your families must have been families of rascals.'

The Jewish priest could retort further. He would say that there are misfortunes attached to human nature, and others sent expressly by god. But one would make this argufier see how ridiculous it is to think that fever and hail are now a divine punishment, and now a natural effect.

Finally the Pharisees and the Essenes, among the Jews, accepted a belief in a hell in their manner. This dogma had already passed from the Greeks to the Romans, and was adopted by the Christians.

Several church fathers did not believe in eternal punishment: it appeared to them absurd to burn a poor wretch throughout eternity because he had stolen a goat. Virgil can say in the sixth book of the *Aeneid*:

> . . . *Sedet aeternumque sedebit*
> *Infelix Theseus.*
> [Wretched Theseus sits and shall for ever sit.]

He implies in vain that Theseus is seated forever on a chair, and that this position constitutes his torment. Others believed that Theseus is a hero who is not seated in hell, but that he is in the Elysian fields.

Not long ago a good and decent Protestant minister preached and wrote that the damned would one day be pardoned, that the suffering should be proportionate to the sin, and that the error of a moment cannot deserve infinite punishment. The priests, his colleagues, dismissed this indulgent judge. One said to him: 'My dear fellow, I don't believe any more than you do that hell is eternal; but it's a good thing for your maid, your tailor, and even your lawyer to believe it.'

Idol, idolator, idolatry

Idol comes from the Greek εἶδος, form; εἴδωλον, representation of a form; λατρεύειν, to serve, revere, adore. This word adore is Latin, and has many different meanings: it signifies putting a hand to one's mouth when speaking with respect, bowing, kneeling, saluting, and finally, most generally, offering a supreme worship. Nothing but ambiguities.

It is useful to note here that the *Dictionnaire de Trévoux* begins its article by saying that all pagans were idolators, and that the Indians are still idolatrous peoples. First of all, no one was called a pagan before Theodosius the younger. This name was then given to the inhabitants of the Italian cities, *pagorum incolae, pagani* [rustics], who kept to their ancient religion. In the second place, Hindustan is Mohammedan, and the Mohammedans are the implacable enemies of images and idolatry. In the third place, many Indian peoples belong to the ancient religion of the Parsees and should not be called idolators, any more than certain castes which have no idols.

Inquiry Whether There Has Ever Been an Idolatrous Government

It would appear that no people on earth has taken this name of idolator. The word is an insult, a term of abuse, like that of *gavaches* [cowards], which the Spaniards once applied to the French, and that of *maranes* [Moors], which the French applied to the Spaniards. Had one asked the Roman senate, the Greek areopagus, the court of the kings of Persia: 'Are you idolators?' they would hardly have understood the question. None would have answered: 'We worship images, idols.' This word 'idolator', 'idolatry', is not found in Homer nor in Hesiod nor in Herodotus nor in any author of the religion of the gentiles. There has never been any edict, any law that ordered men to worship idols, to serve them as gods, to regard them as gods.

When the Roman and Carthaginian leaders made a treaty, they invoked all their gods. 'It is in their presence,' they said, 'that we swear peace.' Now the statues of all these gods, whose number was very great, were not in the generals' tents. They considered the gods to be present at men's actions as witnesses and judges. And it was certainly not the simulacrum that constituted the divinity.

What view did they then take of the statues of their false divinities in the temples? The same view, if I may say so, that we take of the images of the objects of our veneration. The error was not to worship a piece of wood or marble, but to worship a false divinity represented by this wood or marble. The difference between them and us is not that they had images and we have not: the difference is that their images showed fantastic beings in a religion. The Greeks had the statue of Hercules, and we have that of saint Christopher; they had Aesculapius and his goat, and we have saint Roch and his dog: they had Jupiter armed with thunder, and we saint Anthony of Padua and saint James of Compostella.

When the consul Pliny, in the opening of his panegyric of Trajan, addresses his prayers *to the immortal gods*, he does not address himself to images. These images were not immortal.

Neither the last days of paganism nor the most ancient offer a single fact enabling us to conclude that an idol was worshipped. Homer speaks only of the gods who inhabit high Olympus. The *palladium*, although fallen from heaven, was only a sacred pledge of Pallas's protection: it was she who was venerated in the *palladium*.

But the Romans and the Greeks kneeled down before statues, gave them crowns, incense, flowers, paraded them in triumph in public places. We have sanctified these customs, and we are no idolators.

In times of drought, women, having fasted, carried the statues of the gods. They walked barefoot, their hair dishevelled, and the rain at once came down in pailfuls, as Petronius says, *et statim urceatim pluebat*. Have we not consecrated this practice, illegal among the gentiles and undoubtedly legitimate with us? In how many villages are the reliquaries of the saints not carried barefoot to obtain the blessings of heaven through their intercession? If a Turk or an educated Chinese were to witness these ceremonies, he could, not knowing better, at first accuse us of putting our trust in the images we thus parade in procession: but a word would undeceive him.

One is surprised by the prodigious number of declamations poured out at all periods against the idolatry of the Romans and the Greeks; and then one is even more surprised when it is realized that they were not idolators.

Some temples were more privileged than others. The great Diana of Ephesus had a higher reputation than a village Diana. More miracles were performed in the temple of Aesculapius at Epidaurus than in some other of his temples. The statue of the Olympian Jupiter attracted more offerings than that of the Paphlagonian Jupiter. But, since here we must always contrast the custom of a true religion with those of a false religion, have we not had for several centuries more devotion at certain altars than at others? Do we not take more offerings to Notre Dame of Loretto than to Notre Dame of the snows? It is for us to determine whether this pretext should be seized on to accuse us of idolatry.

Only a single Diana, a single Apollo, a single Aesculapius had been conceived, not as many Apollos, Dianas and Aesculapiuses as they had temples and statues. It is thus proved, so far as a point of history can be, that the ancients did not believe that a statue was a divinity, that worship could be transferred to this statue, this idol. It follows that the ancients were not idolators.

A coarse and superstitious rabble which did not reason, which did not know how to doubt, to deny, to believe, which ran to the temples because it was idle and because there the humble were the equals of the great, which brought its offerings out of habit, which talked continually of miracles without having ever investigated one, and which hardly rose above the victims it brought, this rabble, I repeat, might well have been struck by religious dread at the sight of the great Diana and of Jupiter the thunderer, and have unknowingly worshipped the statue itself. This is what has sometimes happened to our rough peasants in our temples; and they are then instructed that it is the intercession of the blessed, the immortals received into heaven, they must seek, and not that of wooden and stone images.

The Greeks and Romans increased the number of their gods by apotheoses. The Greeks deified conquerors like Bacchus, Hercules, Perseus. Rome erected altars to its emperors. Our apotheoses are of a different kind: we have saints instead of their demi-gods, their secondary gods, but we respect neither rank nor conquests. We have raised temples to men who were simply virtuous, who for the most part would be unknown on earth were they not placed in heaven. The apotheoses of the ancients were procured by flattery, ours by respect for virtue.

In his philosophical works Cicero offers not the slightest suspicion that the statues of the gods could be misunderstood and confounded with the gods themselves. His interlocutors fulminated against the established religion, but not one of them took it into his head to accuse the Romans of regarding marble and brass as divinities. Lucretius does not reproach anyone with this foolishness, he also reproaches the superstitious with everything. Therefore, once again, this opinion did not exist, there was no notion of it, there were no idolators.

Horace makes a statue of Priapus say: 'I was once the trunk of a fig tree. A carpenter, doubtful whether to make me into a god or a bench, finally decided to make me a god, etc.' What should we conclude from this pleasantry? Priapus was one of those little subordinate divinities, given up to the mockers; and this pleasantry is itself the strongest evidence that the image of Priapus, which was erected in the kitchen garden to frighten the birds, was not highly revered.

Adopting the attitude of a commentator, Dacier did not fail to point out that Baruch had predicted this incident when he said: 'They will be only what the workman wishes'; but he might also have remarked that as much can be said of all statues. Is it to be supposed that Baruch had a vision about the satires of Horace?

A wash-basin can be just as easily drawn from a block of marble as an image of Alexander or of Jupiter or of something else more respectable. The material from which the cherubim of the holy of holies were formed could have served equally well for the basest functions. Is a throne or an altar less revered because the workman could have made it into a kitchen table?

Instead of concluding that the Romans worshipped the statue of Priapus, and that Baruch had predicted it, Dacier should therefore have concluded that the Romans made fun of it. Consult all the authors who refer to the statues of their gods. You will not find one who talks of idolatry. They say expressly the contrary. In Martial you find:

Qui finxit sacros auro vel marmore vultus,
Non facit ille deos; . . .
[He does not make gods who forms sacred
images in gold or marble.]

In Ovid:

Colitur pro Jove forma Jovis.
[In the image of Jupiter, Jupiter is worshipped.]

In Statius:

Nulla autem effigies, nulli commissa metallo
Forma dei; mentes habitare ac numina gaudet.
[God's form is not fixed by statues or metal, he
chooses to live in our minds and hearts.]

In Lucan:

Estne dei sedes, nisi terra et pontus et aer?
[What is god's home if not earth and sea and air?]

One could make a volume of all the passages which
testify that images were merely images.

Only those cases in which statues issued oracles might
have given rise to the idea that these statues had something divine in them. But the prevailing opinion certainly
was that the gods had chosen certain altars, certain
simulacra, in which to dwell occasionally in order to give
audience to humans, and to answer them.

In Homer and the choruses of the Greek tragedies we

find only prayers to Apollo, who delivers his oracles on the mountains, in this temple, in that city. In all antiquity there is not the slightest trace of a prayer addressed to a statue.

Those who practised magic, who believed it to be a science or pretended to believe it, claimed to know how to make the gods descend into their statues – not the great gods, but the secondary ones, the genii. This is what Mercury Trismegistus called *making gods*, and what saint Augustine refuted in his *City of God*. But this in itself shows clearly that the simulacra had nothing divine in them, since it was necessary for a magician to animate them. And it seems to me that a magician very seldom had the skill to give a statue a soul, to make it speak.

In a word, the images of the gods were not gods. Jupiter, and not his image, hurled the thunder; it was not the statue of Neptune that raised the seas; nor that of Apollo which gave us light. The Greeks and the Romans were gentiles, polytheists, but not idolators.

Whether the Persians, the Sabaeans, the Egyptians, the Tartars, the Turks were Idolators, and How Ancient is the Origin of the Simulacra Called Idols. History of Their Worship

It is a great mistake to describe as idolators peoples who worshipped the sun and the stars. For a long time these nations had neither simulacra nor temples. If they were in error it was in devoting to the stars what they should have devoted to the creator of the stars. In any case, the dogma of Zoroaster or Zerdust, collected in the *Sadder*, proclaims a supreme being, who avenged and rewarded, which is very far from idolatry. The government of China has never had any idol; it has always preserved the simple worship of the master of heaven, King-tien. Among the Tartars Genghis Khan was not an idolator and had no simulacra. The Moslems who filled Greece, Asia Minor, Syria, Persia, India and Africa, called the Christians idolators, *giaours*, because they believed that the Christians worshipped images. They smashed several statues they found in Constantinople in Santa Sophia, in the church of the holy apostles, and in others which they converted into mosques. Appearances misled them as they always mislead mankind, and led them to believe that temples dedicated to saints who had once been men, images of these saints revered on bended knee, miracles performed in these temples, were invincible proof of the most complete idolatry. Nothing of the kind. Christians in fact worship only one god, and revere in the blessed only the quality of god itself operating in his saints. Iconoclasts and Protestants have levelled the same reproach of idolatry against the church, and have been given the same answer.

As men have very seldom had precise ideas, and have even more rarely expressed their ideas in precise and unequivocal words, we applied the name of idolators to the gentiles, and above all to polytheists. Huge volumes have been written, varied notions have been retailed about the origin of this worship of god or of several gods in visible form. This multitude of books and opinions proves only ignorance.

We do not know who invented clothes and footwear, and we want to know who first invented idols. What does a passage in Sanchuniathon matter? He lived before the Trojan war. What does he tell us when he says that chaos, spirit, that is breath, in love with its principles, derived the primal clay from it and made the air luminous, that the wind Colp and his wife Bau begot Eon, that Eon begot Genos, that Chronos, their descendant, had two eyes at the back of his head as well as in front, that he became god, and gave Egypt to his son Thaut? Such is one of the most respectable monuments of antiquity.

Orpheus, earlier than Sanchuniathon, teaches us no more in his *Theogony*, preserved for us by Damascius. He presents the principle of the world in the shape of a dragon with two heads, one a bull's, the other a lion's, with a face in the middle which he calls *god-face*, and gilded wings at the shoulders.

But two great truths can be drawn from these bizarre ideas: one, that visible images and hieroglyphs date from the greatest antiquity; the other, that all the ancient philosophers recognized a first principle.

As for polytheism, good sense will tell you that ever since there have been men, that is, weak animals, capable of reason and folly, subject to every accident, to illness and to death, these men have felt their weakness and their dependence. They have readily recognized that there is something more powerful than they. They have felt a power in the earth that supplies their nourishment, one in the air that often destroys them, one in the fire that consumes and in the water that submerges. What more natural than for ignorant men to imagine beings who preside over these elements? What more natural than to revere the invisible power that makes the sun and the stars shine in our eyes? And, as soon as man sought to form an idea of these powers superior to him, what even more natural than to represent them in a visible manner? Could they ever have done otherwise? The Jewish religion, which preceded ours, and which was given by god himself, was filled with these images by which god is represented. He deigned to speak human language in a bush; he appeared on a mountain; the celestial spirits he sent all came in human shape; finally, the sanctuary is filled with cherubim, which are human bodies with the wings and the heads of animals. This is what led Plutarch, Tacitus, Appian and so many more wrongly to reproach the Jews for worshipping the head of an ass. Although he forbade the painting or carving of any image, god thus deigned to adapt himself to human weakness, which required images to speak to the senses.

Isaiah, in chapter vi, sees the lord seated on a throne, the train of his robe filling the temple. The lord extended his hand and touched Jeremiah's mouth in this prophet's first chapter. Ezekiel, in chapter iii, saw a sapphire throne, and god appeared to him as a man seated on this throne. These images did not corrupt the purity of the Jewish religion, which never used pictures, statues, idols to represent god to the eyes of the people.

The educated Chinese, the Parsees, the ancient Egyptians had no idols, but images of Isis and Osiris soon appeared, soon Bel became a great colossus in Babylon. Brahma was a bizarre monster in the Indian archipelago.

Above all the Greeks multiplied the names of the gods, the statues and the temples, but always attributing the supreme power to their Zeus, called Jupiter by the Latins, master of the gods and of men. The Romans imitated the Greeks. These peoples always placed all the gods in the sky, without knowing what they meant by sky.

The Romans had their twelve great gods, six male and six female, whom they named *dii maiorum gentium*: Jupiter, Neptune, Apollo, Vulcan, Mars, Mercury, Juno, Vesta, Minerva, Ceres, Venus, Diana. Pluto was then forgotten. Vesta took his place.

Then came the gods *minorum gentium*: the local deities, the heroes, like Bacchus, Hercules, Aesculapius; the infernal gods, Pluto, Proserpine; those of the sea, like Thetis, Amphitrite, the Nereids, Glaucus; then the Dryads, the Naiads; the gods of the garden, those of the shepherds. There was a god for every profession, for every activity, for children, for nubile girls, for married women, for women in childbed. They had the god Fart. Finally they deified the emperors. But in fact neither these emperors, nor the god Fart, nor the goddess Pertunda, nor Priapus, nor Rumilia the goddess of tits, nor Stercutius the god of the privy, were regarded as the masters of heaven and earth. The emperors sometimes had temples, the minor household gods had none; but all had their images, their idols. These were little figurines with which a man decorated his study. They were the amusements of old women and children, not authorized by any public worship. The superstition of every private person was indulged. These little idols are still found in the ruins of ancient cities.

Though nobody knows when men started to make idols, we know that they are of the highest antiquity. Terah, Abraham's father, made them at Ur in Chaldea. Rachel stole and carried off the idols of her father-in-law Laban. It is impossible to go further back than that.

But what precise notion did the ancient nations have of all these simulacra? What virtue, what power, was attributed to them? Was it believed that the gods descended from heaven to hide themselves in these statues, or that they communicated to them a part of the divine spirit, or that they communicated nothing at all to them? This too has been the subject of much useless writing. It is obvious that each man judged it according to the degree of his reason or his credulity or his fanaticism. It is evident that the priests attached as much divinity as they could to their statues in order to attract more offerings to themselves. We know that the philosophers condemned these superstitions, that the warriors made fun of them, that the magistrates tolerated them, and the people, always absurd, did not know what it was doing. This, in a few words, is the history of all the nations to whom god has not made himself known.

One can gather the same notion about the worship all Egypt gave to an ox, and that several cities gave to a dog, to a monkey, to a cat, to onions. It would seem that these were at first emblems. Then a certain ox Apis, a certain dog called Anubis, were worshipped. They still ate beef, and onions, but it is hard to know what the old women of Egypt thought of sacred onions and oxen.

The idols spoke quite often. The elegant words spoken by the statue of Cybele when it was removed from the palace of king Attalus were commemorated in Rome on the feast day of that goddess.

Ipsa peti volui; ne sit mora, mitte volentem:
Dignus Roma locus quo deus omnis eat.

I wanted to be carried off, take me quickly away;
Rome is worthy to be the home of every god.

The statue of Fortune had spoken. It is true that the Scipios, the Ciceros, the Caesars did not believe this, but the old woman to whom Encolpius gave a crown to buy geese and gods may well have believed it.

The idols also uttered oracles, and the priests, hidden in the hollow statues, spoke in the name of the divinity.

In the midst of so many gods and so many different theogonies and individual cults, why is it that there was never any war of religion among the peoples called idolators? This peace was a good born of an evil, of error itself. For each nation, recognizing several inferior gods, thought it right that neighbouring peoples should also have theirs. Except Cambyses, who is reproached for having killed the ox Apis, we do not find in profane history any conqueror who maltreated the gods of a vanquished people. The gentiles had not a single exclusive religion, and the priests thought only of multiplying the offerings and the sacrifices.

The first offerings were fruits. Soon after, animals were needed for the priests' table; they slaughtered them themselves; they became butchers, and cruel; finally they introduced the horrible practice of sacrificing human victims, and above all children and virgins. Neither the Chinese nor the Parsees nor the Indians were ever guilty of these abominations, but according to Porphyry men were immolated at Hieropolis, in Egypt.

In Tauris foreigners were sacrificed. Fortunately the priests of Tauris could not have much practice. The first Greeks, the Cypriots, the Phoenicians, the Tyrians, the Carthaginians had this abominable superstition. The Romans themselves fell into this religious crime, and Plutarch reports that they immolated two Greeks, and two Gauls to expiate the love affairs of three vestals. Procopius, contemporary of the king of the Franks Theodobert, tells us that the Franks immolated men when they entered Italy with this prince. The Gauls, the Germans commonly made these frightful sacrifices. It is hardly possible to read history without conceiving a horror of mankind.

It is true that, among the Jews, Jephtah sacrificed his daughter, and Saul was prepared to immolate his son. It is true that those who were dedicated to the lord by anathema could not be bought back as animals were bought back, and had to perish. Samuel, a Jewish priest, chopped into pieces with a sacred hatchet king Agag, a prisoner of war whom Saul had pardoned, and Saul was condemned for observing the law of nations with this king. But god, master of men, can take their lives when he pleases, how he pleases, and by the hand of whom he pleases; and it is not for men to put themselves in the place of the master of life and death, and to usurp the rights of the supreme being.

To console mankind for this horrible spectacle, these

pious sacrileges, it is important to know that among nearly all the nations called idolators there was sacred theology and popular error, the secret cult and public ceremonies, the religion of the wise and that of the vulgar. Only one god was taught in the mysteries to the initiates. One has only to glance at the hymn, attributed to the ancient Orpheus, which was sung in the mysteries of Ceres Eleusinus, so famous in Europe and Asia: 'Contemplate divine nature, illuminate your spirit, govern your heart, walk in the path of justice. May the god of heaven and earth be always present to your eyes. He is unique, he exists in himself alone. All beings derive their existence from him. He sustains them all. He has never been seen by mortals, and he sees all things.'

Read also this passage from the philosopher Maximus of Madaurus in his *Letter to Saint Augustine*: 'What man is gross and stupid enough to doubt that there is a supreme, eternal, infinite god who has begotten nothing like himself, and who is the common father of all things.'

A thousand passages testify that wise men abhorred not only idolatry, but also polytheism.

Epictetus, this model of resignation and patience, this man who was so great in so low a condition, never speaks of anything but a single god. Here is one of his maxims: 'God has created me, god is within me, I bear him everywhere. Could I soil him by obscene thoughts, unjust actions, infamous desires? My duty is to thank god for all, to praise him for all, and to cease from blessing him only when I cease to live.' All the ideas of Epictetus turn on this principle. Is he an idolator?

Marcus Aurelius, perhaps as great on the throne of

the Roman empire as Epictetus in slavery, often speaks, it is true, of the gods, whether to conform to accepted language, or to refer to beings intermediate between the supreme being and men. But in how many places does he not show that he recognizes only one eternal, infinite god! 'Our soul,' he says, 'is an emanation of the divinity. My children, my body, my wits come to me from god.'

The Stoics, the Platonists acknowledged a divine and universal nature. The Epicureans denied it. The pontiff spoke of only one god in the mysteries. Where then were the idolators? All our phrase-mongers proclaim idolatry as little dogs yap when they hear a big dog bark.

For the rest, it is one of the great mistakes of Moréri's dictionary to say that at the time of Theodosius idolators were left only in the distant countries of Asia and Africa. Even in the seventh century there were still many gentile peoples in Italy. North Germany, beyond the Weser, was not Christian in Charlemagne's time. Poland and all the north remained long after him in what is called idolatry. Half of Africa, all the kingdoms beyond the Ganges, Japan, the common people of China, a hundred hordes of Tartars preserved their ancient cult. In Europe only a few Laplanders, Samoyedes, Tartars have persevered in the religion of their ancestors.

I conclude by noting that in the times we name the middle ages, we called the country of the Moham-medans heathendom. We qualified as idolators, image-worshippers, a people who have a horror of images. We must admit once more that the Turks would be more pardonable to take us for idolators when they see our altars loaded with images and statues.

Joseph

The story of Joseph, considered merely as a curiosity and as literature, is one of the most precious monuments of antiquity to have come down to us. It appears to be the model for all oriental writers. It is more affecting than Homer's *Odyssey*, for a hero who pardons is more touching than one who avenges himself.

We regard the Arabs as the first authors of those ingenious fictions that have passed into all languages; but I see in them no adventure comparable to Joseph's. Nearly everything in it is marvellous, and the end brings a lump to the throat. Here we have a young man of sixteen whose brothers are jealous. They sell him to a caravan of Ishmaelite merchants, he is taken to Egypt, and bought by one of the king's eunuchs. This eunuch had a wife, which is not at all surprising. The Kislar-aga, a complete eunuch, who has had everything cut off, has a harem today in Constantinople. He was left his eyes and his hands, and nature has not lost its rights in his heart. The other eunuchs, who have had cut off only the two accompaniments of the organ of generation, still use that organ frequently, and Potiphar, to whom Joseph was sold, may very well have been one of those eunuchs.

The wife of Potiphar fell in love with the young Joseph, who, faithful to his master and benefactor, rejected the woman's attentions. This irritated her, and she accused Joseph of trying to seduce her. It is the story of Hippolytus and Phaedra, Bellerophon and Stheneboea, Hebrus and Damasippa, Tanis and Peribea, Myrtil and Hippodamia, Peleus and Demenette.

It is difficult to know which of all these stories is the original. But in the ancient Arabic authors the adventure of Joseph and Potiphar's wife contains a very ingenious touch. The author imagines that Potiphar, undecided between his wife and Joseph, did not consider Joseph's tunic, which his wife had torn, to be proof of the young man's attack. There was a child in a cradle in the woman's room. Joseph said that she had torn and removed his tunic in the child's presence. Potiphar consulted the child, whose intelligence was very developed for its age. The child said to Potiphar: 'See whether the tunic is torn in front or behind: if in front this is evidence that Joseph tried to violate your wife, who defended herself; if behind it is evidence that your wife was running after him.' Thanks to this child's genius, Potiphar recognized the innocence of his slave. This is how the adventure is recounted in the *Koran* after the ancient Arabic author. He is not concerned to tell us to whom belonged the child who judged with so much intelligence. If it was the son of Potiphar's wife, Joseph was not the first she had pursued.

Be that as it may, according to *Genesis* Joseph was imprisoned, and found himself in company with the Egyptian king's cup-bearer and baker. These two prisoners of state dreamed during the night. Joseph explained their dreams, predicting that in three days the cup-bearer would be restored to favour, and the baker hung: which is what came to pass.

Two years later the king of Egypt also dreamed. His cup-bearer told him that there was a young Jew in prison who understood dreams better than anyone else in the world. The king sent for the young man, who predicted seven years of plenty and seven years of want.

Let us here briefly interrupt the thread of the story to consider how prodigiously ancient is the interpretation of dreams. Jacob had seen in a dream the mysterious ladder that led to god himself. He learned in a dream a way to multiply his flocks, a way that succeeded only for him. Joseph himself had learned in a dream that he would one day dominate his brothers. Long before, Abimelech had been warned in a dream that Sarah was the wife of Abraham.

Let us return to Joseph. As soon as he had explained Pharaoh's dream, he became prime minister on the spot. We may doubt whether a king could be found nowadays, even in Asia, who would bestow such an office for the explanation of a dream. Pharaoh made Joseph marry one of Potiphar's daughters. It is said that this Potiphar was the high priest of Heliopolis. So this was not his first master the eunuch, or if it was he, he was certainly entitled to be called something else in addition to high priest, and his wife had been a mother more than once.

In the meanwhile famine came as Joseph had predicted, and Joseph, to deserve the marked favour of his king, obliged everybody to sell their land to Pharaoh, and the entire nation enslaved itself to get grain. This was apparently the origin of despotic power. It must be admitted that never had a king made a better bargain, but the people can hardly have blessed the prime minister.

Finally Joseph's father and brothers also needed grain, for 'the famine was sore in all the earth'. It is hardly necessary to relate here how Joseph received his brothers, how he forgave and enriched them. All that constitutes an interesting epic poem is found in this story: exposition, crux, recognition, vicissitudes and marvels. Nothing bears more clearly the hallmark of oriental genius.

What old Jacob, father of Joseph, replied to Pharaoh, must strongly impress anyone who can read. 'How many are the days of the years of thy life?' asked the king. 'The days of the years of my pilgrimage are 130 years, and I have not yet had one happy day in this short pilgrimage.'

Judea

I have not been to Judea, thank God, and will never go. I have met people of all nationalities who have come back from it. They have all told me that the site of Jerusalem is horrible, that all the surrounding country is stony, that the mountains are naked, that the famous river Jordan is only forty-five feet wide, that the only good province in this country is Jericho. In short, they all repeat saint Jerome, who lived for so long in Bethlehem, and who depicts this land as the scrap-heap of nature. He says that in the summer there is not even water to drink. Nevertheless this country must have appeared to the Jews a delightful spot in comparison with the deserts they had come from. Wretches who had left the Landes to live on the mountains of the Lampourdan [around Bayonne] would praise their new home, and if they hoped to penetrate into the good parts of the Languedoc these would strike them as the promised land.

This is precisely the history of the Jews. Jericho and Jerusalem are Toulouse and Montpellier, and the Sinai desert is the country between Bordeaux and Bayonne. But if the god who conducted the Jews wanted to give them good land, and if these unfortunates had in fact lived in Egypt, why did he not leave them there? The only answers given to this question are theological phrases.

Judea, it is said, was the promised land. God said to Abraham: 'I will give you all this land from the river of Egypt unto the Euphrates.'

Alas! my friends, you have never seen these fertile banks of the Euphrates and the Nile. They fooled you. The masters of the Nile and the Euphrates were, each in his turn, your masters. You have nearly always been slaves. To promise and to perform are two things, my poor Jews. You had an old rabbi who, reading the wise prophecies that foretell for you a land of milk and honey, exclaimed that you had been promised more butter than bread. Do you realize that if the Grand Turk offered me today the lordship of Jerusalem I would spurn it?

On seeing this detestable country Frederick II said publicly that Moses was very ill-advised to lead his company of lepers to it: 'Why didn't he go to Naples?' said Frederick. Good-bye my dear Jews; I am sorry that the promised land should be waste land.

Luxury

For 2,000 years people have declaimed in verse and prose against luxury, and have always loved it.

What has not been said about the earliest Romans, these brigands who ravaged and pillaged the harvests of their neighbours, who destroyed the poor villages of the Volscians and the Samnites in order to aggrandize their own poor village? They were disinterested and virtuous men! They had not yet been able to steal either gold or silver or precious stones, because there was none in the places they sacked. Neither their woods nor their marshes produced partridges or pheasants, and their temperance is praised!

When little by little they had pillaged everything, stolen everything from the far end of the Adriatic to the Euphrates, and had had enough sense to enjoy the fruit of their rapines for seven or eight hundred years, when they cultivated all the arts, tasted every pleasure, and made even the vanquished taste them, then, it is said, they ceased to be wise and upright.

All these declamations come down to proving that a thief must never eat the dinner he has stolen nor wear the clothes he has purloined nor adorn himself with the ring he has taken. All this, it is said, should have been thrown into the river if the thieves wanted to live as honest men. Say rather that one should not steal.

Condemn the brigands when they pillage, but do not call them lunatics when they enjoy what they have taken. Honestly, when a large number of English sailors enriched themselves on taking Pondicherry and Havana, were they wrong to enjoy themselves later in London in return for the pains they had taken at the extremities of Asia and Africa?

Do the windbags want the wealth amassed by the fortunes of war, agriculture, trade and industry to be buried? They instance Lacedaemon. Why do they not cite also the republic of San Marino? Of what benefit was Sparta to Greece? Did she ever have a Demosthenes, Sophocles, Apelles or Phidias? The luxury of Athens produced great men of every kind. Sparta had a few captains, and even those in smaller numbers than the other cities. But so be it! Let a little republic like Lacedaemon preserve its poverty. We attain death just as surely lacking everything as enjoying whatever makes life agreeable. The Canadian savage survives and reaches old age just like the English citizen who has an income of 50,000 guineas. But who will ever compare the country of the Iroquois with England?

Let the republic of Ragusa and the canton of Zug make sumptuary laws. They are right, it is necessary for the poor man not to spend beyond his means, but I have read somewhere:

> *Sachez surtout que le luxe enrichit*
> *Un grand état, s'il en perd un petit.*
> [Know above all that luxury enriches a great state, though it ruins a small one.]

If by luxury you mean excess, everybody knows that excess of every kind is pernicious, in abstinence as in gluttony, in economy as in liberality. I do not know how it has come about that in my villages, in which the land is barren, the taxes heavy, the prohibition against exporting the wheat we have sowed intolerable, there is nevertheless hardly a husbandman without clothes made of good cloth and who is not well shod and well fed. If this farmer cultivates the land in his fine clothes, white linen, curled and powdered hair, that would certainly be the greatest luxury, and the most impertinent. But if a bourgeois of Paris or London appeared in the theatre dressed like this peasant, that would be the crudest and most ridiculous niggardliness.

> *Est modus in rebus, sunt certi denique fines,*
> *Quos ultra citraque nequit consistere rectum.*
> [There is a measure in all things, fixed limits which
> virtue must neither overstep nor fail to attain.]

Scissors are certainly not of the greatest antiquity. When they were invented what was not said against the first who pared their nails and cut part of the hair that fell over their noses? They were no doubt called dandies and prodigals, who bought at a high price a tool of vanity to spoil the work of the creator. What an enormous sin to shorten the horn that god causes to grow at the ends of our fingers! It was an insult to divinity. It was much worse when shirts and socks were invented. We know how furiously the old councillors, who had never worn them, cried out against the young magistrates who yielded to this fatal luxury.

Martyr

We can only guffaw at all the humbug we are told about martyrs. Such men as Titus, Trajan, Marcus Aurelius, these models of virtue, are depicted as monsters of cruelty. Fleury, *abbé* of the Loc-Dieu, dishonoured his ecclesiastical history with stories a sensible woman would not tell to little children.

Can it be seriously repeated that the Romans condemned each of seven virgins of seventy to pass through the hands of all the young men of the city of Ancyra, the same Romans who punished vestals with death for the slightest love-affair? It was apparently to give pleasure to inn-keepers that the story was invented of a Christian inn-keeper called Theodotus, who prayed to god to kill these seven virgins rather than to expose them to the loss of the oldest virginities. God gave ear to the prudish inn-keeper, and the proconsul had the seven misses drowned in a lake. As soon as they were drowned they went to Theodotus to complain of the trick he had played on them, and begged him earnestly to prevent the fishes from eating them. Theodotus took with him three topers from his tavern, marched to the lake with them, preceded by a celestial torch and a celestial horseman, fished up the seven old ladies, buried them, and finished by being hanged.

Diocletian met a little boy called saint Roman, who

stuttered. He wanted to have him burnt because he was a Christian. Three Jews who happened to be there started to laugh because Jesus Christ allowed a little boy who belonged to him to be burnt. They exclaimed that their religion was superior to the Christian since god delivered Shadrach, Meshach and Abednego from the fiery furnace. The flames which enveloped the young Roman without hurting him at once divided and burned the three Jews. The emperor, very astonished, said that he wanted to have no quarrel with god, but a village judge, less scrupulous, condemned the little stutterer to have his tongue cut out. The emperor's chief physician had the decency to perform the operation himself. As soon as he had cut out the little Roman's tongue, the child started to chatter with a volubility that transported the whole assembly with admiration.

A hundred stories of this kind are to be found in the martyrologies. Thinking to make the ancient Romans odious they made themselves ridiculous. Do you want good, well-attested barbarities; good, well-authenticated massacres; rivers of blood that really ran; fathers, mothers, husbands, women, children at the breast really butchered and piled up on each other? Persecuting monsters, seek these truths only in your annals: you will find them in the crusades against the Albigensians, in the massacres of Mérindol and Cabrières, in the appalling day of saint Bartholomew, in the Irish massacres, in the valleys of the Waldenses. It well becomes you, barbarians that you are, to impute extravagant cruelties to the best of emperors, you who have inundated Europe with blood, and covered it with dying bodies, to prove that it is possible to be in a thousand places at once, and that the pope can sell indulgences! Stop slandering the Romans, who gave you your laws, and ask god's forgiveness for the abominations of your fathers.

It is not the suffering, you say, that makes the martyr; it is the cause. Well, I grant that your victims should not be given the name of martyr, which means witness. But what name shall we give your executioners? Phalaris and Busiris were the gentlest of men compared with you. Does not your inquisition, which still survives, make reason, nature, religion shudder? Good god! if this infernal tribunal were reduced to ashes, would your vengeful gaze be displeased?

Miracles

A miracle, in the full meaning of the word, is an admirable thing. In this sense everything is miraculous. The prodigious order of nature, the rotation of 100 million globes around a million suns, the activity of light, the life of animals are perpetual miracles.

By conventional usage we call miracle the violation of these divine and eternal laws. If there is an eclipse of the sun at full moon, if a dead man walks two leagues carrying his head in his arms, we call that a miracle.

Several natural philosophers maintain that in this sense there are no miracles; and here are their arguments.

A miracle is the violation of the divine, immutable, eternal laws of mathematics. By this very definition a miracle is a contradiction in terms. A law cannot be at once immutable and violated. But, they are asked, cannot god suspend a law established by himself? They have the hardihood to answer that it cannot, that it is impossible for a being infinitely wise to have made laws in order to violate them. He could disturb his machine, they say, only to make it function better. Now it is clear that this immense machine is as good as he; being god, he could make it: if he saw that there would be imperfection because of the nature of the material, he dealt with it from the beginning; therefore he will never change anything in it.

Besides, god cannot do anything without a reason; and what reason could lead him to disfigure his own work for a time? They will be told that it is for the benefit of mankind. They reply that it must then be for the benefit of all men, for it is impossible to conceive that the divine nature would work for a few individual men, and not for the entire human species. In any case, the human species is not up to much: it is much less than a small ant-hill in comparison with all the beings that fill immensity. Now is it not the most absurd of follies to imagine that the infinite being would invert the eternal play of the immense engines which move the entire universe for the sake of three or four hundred ants on this little heap of mud?

But let us suppose that god wanted to distinguish a small number of men by particular favours: would he have to change what he established for ever and for everywhere? He certainly has not the least need for such a change, for such inconstancy, to favour his creatures: his favours are in his very laws. He has foreseen everything, arranged everything for them: all obey irrevocably the power he has impressed for ever on nature.

Why should god perform a miracle? To accomplish a given plan for a few living beings? He would then be saying: 'I have been unable to accomplish a certain plan by the manufacture of the universe, by my divine decrees, my eternal laws. I am going to change my eternal ideas, my immutable laws to try to perform what I could not accomplish with them.' It would be a confession of his weakness, and not of his power. It would seem to be the most inconceivable contradiction in him. Hence it is really to insult him (if men can insult god) to dare to attribute miracles to him, it is to say to him: 'You are a weak and inconsistent being.' It is therefore absurd to believe in miracles, it is as it were to dishonour the divinity.

These philosophers are pressed, they are told: 'You exalt in vain the immutability of the supreme being, the eternity of his laws, the regularity of his infinite worlds. Our little mud heap has seen an abundance of miracles, history is as full of prodigies as of natural events. The daughters of the high priest Anius changed whatever they chose into wheat, wine or oil. Athalida, daughter of Mercury, resuscitated several times. Aesculapius resuscitated Hippolytus. Hercules dragged Alcestis back from death. Heres returned to the world after passing a fortnight in hell. The parents of Romulus and Remus were a god and a vestal virgin. The Palladium fell from heaven in the city of Troy. The hair of Berenice became a constellation. The hut of Baucis and Philemon was changed into a superb temple. The head of Orpheus rendered oracles after his death. The walls of Thebes were built by the sound of a flute alone, in the presence of the Greeks. The cures performed in the temple of Aesculapius were innummerable, and we still have monuments covered with the names of the eye-witnesses of the miracles of Aesculapius.'

Give me the name of one people among whom incredible prodigies were not performed, especially when few knew how to read and write.

Freethinkers answer these objections only by laughing and shrugging their shoulders. But Christian philosophers say: 'We believe in the miracles operated in our holy religion. We believe them by faith and not by reason, to which we take great care not to listen, for it is well known that the reason must not utter a single word when faith speaks. We have a firm and entire belief in the miracles of Jesus Christ and the apostles, but you must permit us to doubt a little about some others. Permit us, for instance, to suspend our judgement about the story told by a simple man to whom the name of great has been given. He asserts that a little monk was so much accustomed to perform miracles that the prior finally forbade him to exercise his talent. The little monk obeyed; but, having seen a poor tiler falling from the top of a roof, he hesitated between the wish to save his life and holy obedience. He simply ordered the tiler to remain in the air until further notice, and ran to tell his prior how things stood. The prior gave him absolution of the sin he had committed in beginning a miracle without permission, and allowed him to finish it, provided that he stopped there and did not do it again. We agree with freethinkers that this story must be distrusted a little.'

But how do you dare to deny, they will be asked, that saint Gervase and saint Protasius appeared in a dream to saint Ambrose, and told him where their relics were to be found? that saint Ambrose unearthed them, and that they cured a blind man? Saint Augustine was then in Milan. It is he who reports this miracle. *Immenso populo teste*, says he in the *City of God*, Chapter XXII. This is one of the best attested miracles. Freethinkers say that they do not believe a word of it, that Gervase and Protasius appeared to nobody, that it matters very little to mankind whether the whereabouts of the remnants of their carcasses be known or not, that they have no more faith in this blind man than in Vespasian's, that it is a useless miracle, that god does nothing useless; and they hold firmly to their principles. My respect for saint Gervase and saint Protasius does not permit me to share the opinion of these freethinkers. I merely report their incredulity. They make much of the passages in Lucian, in his *Death of Peregrinus*: 'When a deft juggler becomes a Christian he is bound to make his way.' But as Lucian is a profane author he should have no authority for us.

These freethinkers cannot bring themselves to believe the miracles operated in the second century. It is in vain that eye-witnesses write that saint Polycarp, bishop of Smyrna, having been condemned to be burned and thrown into the flames, they heard a heavenly voice crying out: 'Courage, Polycarp! be strong, show yourself a man'; that the flames of the pyre then parted from the body and formed a tent of fire above his head, and a dove came out of the midst of the pyre. At last they had to cut off Polycarp's head. 'What was the good of this miracle?' ask the incredulous. 'Why did the flames lose their nature, and not the executioner's axe? Why is it that so many martyrs have emerged safe and sound from boiling oil, and could not resist the edge of the sword?' They answer that it is the will of god. But the freethinkers would have liked to see all this with their own eyes before believing it.

Those who fortify their arguments with knowledge will tell you that the fathers of the church themselves have often admitted that no more miracles were performed in their times. Saint Chrysostom says expressly: 'The extraordinary gifts of the spirit were given even to the unworthy because the church then needed miracles; but today they are no longer given even to the worthy, because the church no longer needs them.' Then he admits that there is no longer anyone who resuscitates the dead, or even who cures the sick.

Saint Augustine himself, despite the miracle of Gervase and Protasius, says in his *City of God*: 'Why are the miracles that used to be performed no longer performed today?' And he gives the same reason: '*Cur, inquiunt, nunc illa miracula quae praedicatis facta esse non fiunt? Possem quidem dicere necessaria prius fuisse quam crederet mundus, ad hoc ut crederet mundus*' ['Why', they ask, 'are the miracles that used to be done, as you boast, not now done? I could say that they were necessary before the world believed, so that the world should believe'].

It is objected to the freethinkers that saint Augustine, in spite of this admission, nevertheless mentions an old cobbler of Hippo who, having lost his clothes, went to pray in the chapel *of the twenty martyrs*. When he returned he found a fish in whose body was a gold ring, and the cook who prepared the fish said to the cobbler: 'This is what the twenty martyrs give you.'

To this the freethinkers answer that nothing in this story contradicts the laws of nature, that natural laws are not in the least offended by a fish who swallows a gold ring, and a cook who gives this ring to a cobbler, that this is no miracle.

If these freethinkers are reminded that according to

saint Jerome, in his *Life of the Hermit Paul*, this hermit had several conversations with satyrs and fauns, that a raven brought him every day for thirty years half a loaf for his dinner, and a whole loaf on the day saint Anthony called on him, they could again reply that all this is not absolutely against nature, that satyrs and fauns may have existed, and that in any case since this story is puerile, it has nothing in common with the true miracles of the saviour and of his apostles. Several good Christians have objected to the story by Theodoret about saint Simon Stylites. Many miracles that pass for authentic in the Greek church have been called in question by several Latin ones, just as some Latin miracles have been doubted in the Greek church. Then came the Protestants, who have much ill-treated the miracles of both churches.

A learned Jesuit who preached a long time in the Indies complains that neither his colleagues nor he could ever perform a miracle. Xavier laments in several of his letters that he does not have the gift of tongues. He says that he is nothing but a dumb statue among the Japanese. Nevertheless the Jesuits have written that he resuscitated eight dead people: that's a lot, and we must also take into account that he resuscitated them 5,000 leagues from here. Since then some people have been known to say that the abolition of the Jesuits in France is a much greater miracle than those of Xavier and Ignatius.

Be that as it may, all Christians agree that the miracles of Jesus Christ and the apostles are incontestably veridical, but that we are entitled to doubt with all our strength some miracles done in recent times and which have not been positively authenticated.

For a miracle to be well established one would wish it to be performed in the presence of the Académie des Sciences of Paris, or the Royal Society of London, and the faculty of medicine, supported by a detachment of the regiment of guards to control the crowd of people whose indiscretion might prevent the operation of the miracle.

One day a freethinker was asked what he would say if he saw the sun stop, that is, if the movement of the earth round this body stopped, if all the dead resuscitated, and if the mountains in unison fell into the ocean, the whole to prove some important truth, such as versatile grace. 'What I would say?' answered the freethinker. 'I would turn Manichean; I would say that there is one principle which undoes what the other has done.'

Peter

In Italian, Piero or Pietro; in Spanish, Pedro; in Latin, Petrus; in Greek, Petros; in Hebrew, Cepha.

Why have the successors of Peter had so much power in the west and none in the east? This is like asking why the bishops of Wurzburg and Salzburg assumed regalian rights in times of anarchy, while the Greek bishops have always remained subjects. Time, opportunity, the ambition of some and the weakness of others have done and will do everything in this world.

The common opinion was added to this anarchy, and opinion is the queen of men: not that in reality they have clearly defined opinions, but words take their place.

It is reported in the gospel that Jesus said to Peter: 'I will give unto thee the keys of the kingdom of heaven.' The partisans of the bishop of Rome maintained about the eleventh century that he who gives the greater gives also the lesser, that the heavens envelop the earth, and that, Peter having the keys of the container, had also the keys of the content. If by the heavens be understood all the stars and all the planets, it is evident according to Thomasius, that the keys given to Simon Bar-Jona, called Peter, formed a master-key. If by the heavens be understood the clouds, the atmosphere, the ether, the space in which revolve the planets, there are no locksmiths, according to Meursius, who can make a key for such doors as those.

In Palestine keys were wooden pegs tied with a strap. Jesus said to Bar-Jona: 'Whatsoever thou shalt bind on earth shall be bound in heaven.' The pope's theologians have concluded from this that the popes had received the right to bind people to the oath of fidelity made to their kings, and to unbind them from it, and to dispose as they please of all the kingdoms. It is a magnificent conclusion. In the estates general of France of 1302 the communes said in their petition to the king, that 'Boniface VIII is a b— who believed that god binds and imprisons in heaven what this Boniface binds on earth.' A famous Lutheran in Germany (I think it was Melanchthon) had great difficulty in swallowing that Jesus said to Simon Bar-Jona, Cepha or Cephas: 'Thou art Peter [*Pierre*], and upon this rock [*pierre*] I will build my assembly, my church.' He could not believe that god could have used such a play on words, so extraordinary a jest, and that the power of the pope should be based on a pun.

Peter was thought to have been bishop of Rome, but it is well known that at that time and for long after there was no individual see. Christian society only took shape at about the end of the second century.

It is possible that Peter made the journey to Rome; it is even possible that he was crucified head down, although that was not the practice; but there is no proof of all that. We have a letter under his name in which he says that he is in Babylon: judicious canonists have maintained that by Babylon we should understand

Rome. Hence if he had dated the letter from Rome we could have concluded that it had been written in Babylon. Such inferences have long been drawn, and so has the world been regulated.

There was a saintly man who had been made to pay dearly for a benefice in Rome. This is called simony. He was asked whether he believed that Simon Peter had been in Rome. He answered: 'I don't know about Peter, but Simon certainly has.'

As for Peter personally, it must be admitted that Paul was not the only one who was shocked by his behaviour. He and his successors have often and openly been resisted. Paul bitterly reproached him for eating forbidden flesh, that is, pork, black pudding, hare, eel, ixion and griffin. Peter defended himself by saying that he had seen the heavens open about the sixth hour, and a great cloth descend from the four corners of the sky, filled with eels, quadrupeds and birds, and that the voice of an angel had cried out: 'Kill and eat.' This is apparently the same voice, says Wollaston, that has cried to so many pontiffs: 'Kill everything, and eat the substance of the people.'

Casaubon could not approve the way in which Peter treated the good Ananias and his wife Sapphira. By what right, asks Casaubon, did a Jew, slave of the Romans, order or allow all those who believed in Jesus to sell their inheritance and put the proceeds at his feet? If some Anabaptist in London made his brethren lay all their money at his feet, would he not be arrested as a traitorous seducer, a robber who would infallibly be sent to Tyburn? Was it not horrible to put Ananias to death because, without saying anything, he held back a few crowns for his necessities and those of his wife when he sold his property and gave the money to Peter? His wife arrived when Ananias had only just died. Peter, instead of warning her mercifully that he had just caused her husband to die of an apoplexy for keeping a few oboles, and telling her to take care of herself, made her fall into the trap. He asked whether her husband had given all his money to the saints. The good woman answered yes, and died on the spot. What harshness!

Coringius asks why Peter, who thus killed those who gave him alms, did not rather kill all the theologians who had caused the death of Jesus Christ, and had him scourged more than once. O Peter! you kill two Christians who gave you alms, and you allow to live those who crucified your god!

Coringius evidently was not living in any of the homes of the inquisition when he put these daring questions. Erasmus noticed a very peculiar thing in connection with Peter: it is that the head of the Christian religion began his apostolate by denying Jesus Christ, and that the first pontiff of the Jews had begun his ministry by making a golden calf, and worshipping it.

Be that as it may, Peter is depicted as a poor man who catechized the poor. He is like those founders of orders who lived in indigence, and whose successors have become great lords.

The pope, Peter's successor, now won, now lost; but apart from his immediate subjects, about 50 million men on earth remain to him, subject in various ways to his laws.

To acknowledge a master three or four hundred leagues away; to wait before you think until that man has seemed to think; dare to give a final verdict only through commissioners appointed by this foreigner in a law-suit between your own fellow citizens; not dare to take possession of the fields and vineyards secured from one's own king without paying considerable sums to this foreign master; violate the laws of one's country, which prohibit a man from marrying his niece, yet does so legitimately by giving his foreign master a still greater sum; not dare to cultivate one's field on whatever day this foreigner requires one to celebrate the memory of an unknown whom he has sent to heaven by his private authority: this is part of what it means to acknowledge a pope, these are the liberties of the Gallican church.

Some other peoples carry their submission further. In our own day we have seen a sovereign ask the pope's permission to have some monks accused of parricide tried by his royal tribunal, failing to obtain this permission, and not daring to judge them.

It is well known that formerly the rights of the popes went further. They were far above the gods of antiquity, for these gods were merely said to dispose of empires, and the popes really did dispose of them.

Sturbinus says that those who doubt the pope's divinity and infallibility can be forgiven when it is considered:

that forty schisms have profaned the seat of saint Peter, and that twenty-seven have steeped it in blood;

that Stephen VII, son of a priest, disinterred the body of his predecessor Formosus, and had the corpse's head cut off;

that Sergius III, convicted of murders, had a son, by Marozia, who inherited the papacy;

that John X, the lover of Theodora, was strangled in his bed;

that John XI, son of Sergius III, was known only as a debauchee;

that John XII was murdered in his mistress's house;

that Benedict IX bought and resold the pontificate;

that Gregory VII was the initiator of 500 years of civil war sustained by his successors;

that finally, among so many ambitious, bloody and debauched popes, there was an Alexander VI, whose name is spoken with the same horror as that of Nero and Caligula.

It is said that it is evidence of the divine nature of the papacy that it has survived so many crimes; but then the caliphs would have been even more divine had they behaved even more atrociously. This is the reasoning of Dermius, but the Jesuits have answered him.

The philosopher Julian, Roman emperor

Justice is sometimes done very late. Two or three authors, either mercenaries or fanatics, talk about the barbarian and effeminate Constantine as of a god, and call the just, the wise, the great Julian a scoundrel. All the others, who copied the first, repeat the flattery and the calumny. These almost become an article of faith. Finally the time for sound criticism arrives, and, after 1,400 years, enlightened men review the cause that ignorance had judged. Constantine is seen as a man, successful in his ambitions, who laughed at god and at mankind. He had the insolence to pretend that god sent him a heavenly sign which ensured his victory. He soaked himself in the blood of all his family, and went to sleep in sloth; but he was a Christian, and was canonized.

Julian was sober, chaste, disinterested, brave, merciful; but he was not a Christian, and was for long regarded as a monster.

Today, having compared the facts, the documents, Julian's writings and those of his enemies, we are compelled to recognize that although he did not like Christianity it was pardonable for him to hate a sect sullied by the blood of all his family; that having been persecuted, imprisoned, exiled, threatened with death by the Galileans in the reign of the barbarous Constantine, he never persecuted them, that on the contrary he pardoned ten Christian soldiers who had conspired against his life.

We read his letters, and we admire him. 'The Galileans,' he says, 'suffered exile and imprisonment under my predecessor. Those who called each other heretics turn and turn about, massacred each other. I have recalled those they exiled, and freed their prisoners. I have returned their property to the outlawed. I have compelled them to live in peace. But such is the restless rage of the Galileans that they complain because they can no longer devour one another.' What a letter! what a verdict pronounced by philosophy against persecuting fanaticism!

In short, everyone who has studied the facts impartially recognizes that Julian had all the qualities of Trajan, except the inclination for which the Greeks and the Romans have so long been forgiven; all the virtues of Cato, but not his obstinacy and his bad temper; all that we admire in Julius Caesar, and none of his vices; he was as chaste as Scipio. In a word, he was in all things the equal of Marcus Aurelius, the greatest of men.

Nowadays we no longer dare to repeat, after the calumniator Theodoret, that Julian immolated a woman in the temple of Carrhae to propitiate the gods. We no longer repeat that in dying he threw with his hand some drops of his blood towards heaven, saying to Jesus Christ: 'You have vanquished, Galilean!' as if he had fought against Jesus in warring against the Persians; as if this philosopher, who died with so much resignation, had acknowledged Jesus; as if he had believed that Jesus was in the air, and that the air was heaven! These inaptitudes of people who are called fathers of the church are no longer repeated nowadays.

They were finally reduced to ridiculing him, as did the frivolous citizens of Antioch. They reproached him his unkempt beard and the way he walked. But master La Bletterie, you have not seen him walk, and you have read his letters and his laws, monuments of his virtues. What does it matter whether his beard was dirty and his walk hurried, so long as his heart was magnanimous and all his steps tended towards virtue?

One important fact today remains to be examined. Julian is reproached with wanting to falsify Jesus Christ's prophecy by rebuilding the temple of Jerusalem. It is said that fires came out of the ground which prevented the work. It is said that this was a miracle, and that this miracle converted neither Julian, nor Alypius, manager of the enterprise, nor any member of the court. Where-upon the *abbé* de la Bletterie says this: 'He and the philosophers of his court no doubt had recourse to their knowledge of natural philosophy to deprive the divinity of so striking a prodigy. Nature has always been the refuge of the incredulous, but she serves religion so aptly that they ought at least to suspect her of collusion.'

First, it is not true that the gospels say that the Jewish temple would never be rebuilt. It is true that the gospel of *Matthew*, obviously written after the destruction of Jerusalem by Titus, prophesies that not one stone would be left upon another of this temple of the Idumaean Herod. But no evangelist says that it will never be rebuilt. It is quite false that not one stone remained upon another after Titus had it pulled down. He preserved all the foundations, an entire wall, and the Antonia tower.

Secondly, what does it matter to the divinity whether there is a Jewish temple or a powder magazine or a mosque on the spot where the Jews slaughtered oxen and cows?

Thirdly, it is not known whether these alleged fires, which according to some burned the workmen, emanated from the walled enclosure of the city or from that of the temple. But it is difficult to understand why Jesus should have burned the emperor Julian's workmen when he did not burn those of the caliph Omar who, long after, built a mosque on the ruins of the temple, nor those of the great Saladin, who restored this same mosque. Did Jesus have so great a predilection for the mosques of the Moslems?

Fourthly, Jesus, having predicted that not one stone would remain on another in Jerusalem, did not forbid that it be rebuilt.

Fifthly, Jesus predicted several things the accomplishment of which has not been permitted by god. He predicted the end of the world and his advent in the clouds with great power and great majesty at the end of the generation then living. Nevertheless the world still lasts and apparently will last for some time.

Sixthly, if Julian had described this miracle I would have said that he had been deceived by a false and ridiculous report, I would believe that his enemies the Christians spared no effort to oppose his enterprise, that they killed the workmen and made people believe that those workmen had been killed by a miracle. But Julian does not say a word about it. He was busy then with the war against the Persians. He deferred for a time the building of the temple, and died before he could begin it.

Seventhly, this prodigy is reported by Ammianus Marcellinus, who was a pagan. It is very possible that it was interpolated by the Christians: they have been authentically accused of so many others.

But it is no less likely that at a time when people talked of nothing but prodigies and stories of witchcraft, Ammianus Marcellinus should have reported this fable on the word of some credulous mind. Since Titus Livius down to Thou inclusively all histories are tainted by prodigies.

Eighthly, contemporary writers report that at this time there was a great earthquake in Syria, that fire broke out in several places, and that several towns were swallowed up. Thus no miracle remains.

Ninthly, if Jesus worked miracles, would it be to prevent the rebuilding of a temple in which he himself had offered up sacrifices and had been circumcised? Would he not work miracles to Christianize so many nations which jeer at Christianity, or rather to make his Christians gentler and more humane, they who, from Arius and Athanasius to Roland and Cavalier in the Cévennes, have poured out torrents of blood and behaved like cannibals?

From this I conclude that nature is not in *collusion with Christianity*, as La Bletterie says, but that La Bletterie is in collusion with old wives' tales, as Julian says: *Quibus cum stolidis aniculis negotium erat.*

After doing justice to some of Julian's virtues La Bletterie nevertheless ends the history of this great man by saying that his death was a consequence of 'divine vengeance'. If that was so, all heroes who died young were punished by god, from Alexander to Gustavus Adolphus. Julian died the finest of deaths, pursuing his enemies after several victories. Jovian, who succeeded him, reigned a much shorter time than he, and reigned shamefully. I detect no divine vengeance, and I see no more in La Bletterie than a dishonest ranter. But where are the men who dare to speak the truth? The stoic Libanius was one of these rare men. He praised the brave and merciful Julian to Theodosius, the murderer of the Thessalonians, but master Le Beau and master La Bletterie are afraid to praise him to faithful parishioners.

Julian has been reproached because he gave up Christianity, as soon as he could do so without risking his life. This is to reproach a man, taken by thieves and enrolled in their gang with a knife to his throat, for escaping from these brigands. The emperor Constant, no less barbarous than his father Constantine, had soaked himself in the blood of Julian's entire family. He had just killed this great man's blood brother. The empress Eusabia had great difficulty in persuading Constant to allow the young Julian to live. In order not to be murdered this unfortunate prince had to accept a monk's tonsure to ensure and receive what are called the four minor orders. He imitated Junius Brutus, who pretended to be mad in order to outwit Tarquin's fury. He was senseless until the moment when, finding himself in Gaul at the head of an army, he became a man and a great man. This is what is called apostasy by the apostates of reason, if such a term can be applied to those who have never known it.

Montesquieu says: 'Woe to the reputation of any prince who is survived by an enemy faction.' Let us imagine that Julian had completed his victory over the Persians, and that, during a long and peaceful old age, he had seen his ancient religion restored, and Christianity annihilated with the sects of the Pharisees, Sadducees, Rechabites, Essenians, Therapeutes, with the worship of the Syrian goddess, and so many more of which no trace remains – then what praises would all the historians have lavished on Julian! Instead of the epithet of apostate he would have been given that of restorer, and the title of divine would not have seemed exaggerated.

Look at the way all our unworthy compilers of Roman history are on their knees to Constantine and Theodosius, with what baseness they palliate their crimes! Nero certainly never did anything comparable to the massacre of the Thessalonians. The Cantabrian Theodosius pretended to pardon the Thessalonians, and six months later he invited them to games in the municipal circus. This circus had room for at least 15,000 persons, and it is certain that it was full. The people's passion for spectacles is notorious. Fathers and mothers brought children who could hardly walk. As soon as the crowd had arrived, the Christian emperor sent Christian soldiers, who massacred old men, youngsters, women, girls, children, without sparing a single one. And this monster is exalted by all our compiling plagiarists because, they say, he did penance. Good god, what penance! He did not give an obol to the families of the dead. But he did not go to mass. It must be admitted that one suffers horribly when one does not go to mass, that god is infinitely grateful to you for it, that it redeems all crimes.

The infamous continuator of Laurent Echard calls the massacre ordered by Theodosius a vivacity.

The same wretches who scribble Roman history in a bombastic style full of solecisms, tell you that Theodosius, before engaging battle with his rival Eugene, saw saint John and saint Philip dressed in white, who promised him victory. Let such writers sing hymns to John and to Philip, but let them not write history.

Reader, examine your conscience. You admire, you love Henry IV. But if he had fallen at the battle of Arques, where his enemies were ten to one against him, and where he was victorious only because he was a hero in the fullest sense of the word, you would not know him: he would only be the Bearnese, a guerilla, a relapsed heretic, an apostate. The duc de Mayenne would be a man sent by god, the pope would have canonized saint Philip, riddled though he was by the pox, and saint John would have appeared to him more than once. And you, Daniel the Jesuit, how you would have flattered Mayenne in your poor and arid history! how he would have 'pushed after him', how he would always have 'beaten' the Bearnese 'hollow'! how the church would have 'triumphed'!

Careat successibus opto
Quisquis ab eventu facta notanda putaat.
[I beg that he come to naught who thinks
that the deed should be judged by its result.]

Prejudices

A prejudice is an irrational opinion. Thus throughout the world all sorts of opinions are instilled into children before they are able to use judgement.

There are universal and necessary prejudices, which constitute virtue itself. In all countries children are taught to acknowledge a god who rewards and avenges; to respect and love their fathers and mothers; to regard theft as a crime, selfish lying as a vice, before they can imagine what is a vice and a virtue.

There are therefore very good prejudices: they are those ratified by the judgement when one is able to reason.

Feeling is not mere prejudice, it is something much stronger. A mother does not love her son because she has been told that she must love him: she happily cherishes him despite herself. It is not out of prejudice that you run to help an unknown child about to fall into a precipice or to be devoured by an animal.

But it is out of prejudice that you respect a man dressed in a certain way, who behaves solemnly and talks in the same way. Your parents told you that you should bow to this man. You respect him before you know whether he deserves your respect. You grow in age and knowledge. You perceive that this man is a charlatan eaten up with pride, selfishness and guile.

You despise what you revered, and prejudice yields to judgement. Out of prejudice you believed the fables with which your childhood was deluded. You were told that the Titans made war on the gods and that Venus was in love with Adonis. When one is twelve one takes these fables for truths, at twenty-one regards them as ingenious allegories.

Let us examine in a few words the different kinds of prejudices, so as to put our affairs into order. We shall perhaps be like those who, at the time of Law's system, realized that they had been counting on imaginary wealth.

Prejudices of the Senses

Is it not an odd thing that our eyes always deceive us, even when we see very well, but that on the contrary our ears do not deceive us? If your ear is in good order and hears: 'You're beautiful, I love you', it is quite certain that you were not told: 'I hate you, you're ugly.' But you see a smooth mirror, and it has been proved that you are mistaken, that in fact it has a very uneven face. The sun has a diameter of about two feet to your eyes. It has been proved to be a million times bigger than the earth.

It seems that god has put the truth into your ears and error into your eyes; but study optics and you will see that god has not deceived you, and that in the present state of things it is impossible for objects to appear to you otherwise than they do.

Physical Prejudices

The sun rises, so does the moon, the earth is immobile: these are natural prejudices concerning the physical world. But that crayfish are good for the blood because they too are red when boiled; that eels cure paralysis because they quiver; that the moon influences illnesses because it was once observed that a patient's fever increased during the waning of the moon: these notions, and a thousand more, were the errors of ancient charlatans, who concluded without reasoning, and who, being deceived, deceived others.

Historical Prejudices

Most histories have been believed without investigation, and this credulity is a prejudice. Fabius Pictor tells us that several centuries before his time a vestal going to draw water in her pitcher, in the town of Elba, was raped, that she gave birth to Romulus and Remus, that they were suckled by a she-wolf, etc. The Roman people believed this fable. They did not inquire whether there had been vestals in Latium at that time, whether it was credible that the daughter of a king should leave her convent with her pitcher, whether it was probable that a she-wolf should suckle two children instead of eating them. The prejudice established itself.

A monk wrote that Clovis, being in great danger at the battle of Tolbiac, vowed to become a Christian if he got through it safely. But is it natural to address oneself to an alien god at such a time? Is it not then that the religion in which one was born acts most powerfully? What Christian, in a battle against the Turks, would not address himself to the holy virgin rather than to Mohammed? It is also said that a pigeon brought the holy ampulla in its beak for the anointment of Clovis, and that an angel brought the oriflamme to guide him. Prejudice believed all the anecdotes of this kind. Those who know human nature are well aware that the usurper Clovis and the usurper Rolon or Rol became Christians in order more easily to control the Christians, just as the Turkish usurpers became Moslems more easily to control the Moslems.

Religious Prejudices

If your nurse told you that Ceres presides over corn, or that Vishnu and Xaca have several times taken human form, or that Sammonocodom came to cut down a forest, or that Odin is waiting for you in his hall somewhere in Jutland, or that Mohammed or somebody else made a journey into heaven; if then your tutor drove into your brain what your nurse engraved there, you will keep hold of it for life. Should your judgement seek to rise above these prejudices, your neighbours, above all the women, scream impiety and frighten you. Your dervish, fearing to see his income diminish, accuses you to the cadi, and his cadi has you impaled if he can, because he wants to command fools, and believes that fools obey better than others. And that will last until your neighbours and the dervish and the cadi begin to understand that folly is worthless and that persecution is abominable.

Pride

In one of his letters Cicero says familiarly to his friend: 'Let me know to whom you would like me to give Gaul.' In another he complains that he is tired of the letters of various princes who thank him for having had their provinces elevated into kingdoms, and he adds that he does not even know where these kingdoms are.

It may be that Cicero, who of course had often been applauded and obeyed by the Roman people, a people that was sovereign, and who was thanked by kings he did not know, had some impulses of pride and vanity.

Although this feeling is not at all suitable for so puny an animal as man, we might nevertheless pardon it in a Cicero, a Caesar, a Scipio, but that at the far end of one of our semi-barbarous provinces a man who has bought a minor office and printed some mediocre verse, should take it into his head to be proud, that is enough to make us laugh loud and long.

Self-love

A vagabond grandly asked for alms near Madrid. A passer-by said to him: 'Aren't you ashamed to carry on this infamous trade when you can work?' 'Sir,' replied the beggar, 'I am asking for your money, not for advice'; then he turned his back, preserving all his Castilian dignity. This gentleman was a proud vagabond; it took little to wound his vanity. He asked for alms out of self-love, and could not bear to be reprimanded by another self-love.

A missionary travelling in India met a fakir loaded with chains, as naked as a monkey, lying on his stomach, and having himself whipped for the sins of his fellow countrymen the Indians, who gave him a few farthings. 'What self-renunciation!' said one of the spectators. 'Self-renunciation!' answered the fakir. 'Know that I have myself lashed in this world only to pay you back in the other, when you will be horses and I a horseman.'

Those who have said that self-love is the basis of all our feelings and of all our actions were therefore quite right in India, in Spain, and in all the habitable world: and just as no one writes to prove to men that they have faces, there is no need to prove to them that they have self-love. This self-love is the instrument of our conservation; it resembles the instrument that perpetuates the species: it is necessary, it is dear to us, it gives us pleasure, and it must be hidden.

Wicked

We are told loudly that human nature is essentially perverse, that man is born the child of the devil, and wicked. Nothing is more ill-considered. For, old friend, you who preach that the whole world is born perverse, you warn me that you were born thus, that I must distrust you like a fox or a crocodile. 'Not at all!' you tell me, 'I'm regenerated, I'm neither heretical nor infidel, you can trust me.' But the rest of mankind, which is either heretical or what you call infidel, is nothing but an assembly of monsters; and every time you talk to a Lutheran or to a Turk you must feel sure that they will rob and murder you, for they are children of the devil, born wicked, one unregenerated, the other degenerated. It would be much more rational, much more elegant to say to men: *You are all born good; consider how awful it would be to corrupt the purity of your being*. We ought to have behaved to mankind as we behave to every individual man. If a monk leads a scandalous life, we say to him: 'Would you really dishonour the dignity of a monk?' A lawyer is reminded that he has the honour to be a royal councillor, and should give an example. In order to encourage a soldier he is told: 'Remember that you belong to the regiment of Champagne.' Every individual should be told: 'Remember your human dignity.'

And in fact, whatever is said about it, we always come

back to that; for what is the meaning of the saying, so often used in all nations, *search your heart*? If you were born a child of the devil, if your origin were criminal, if your blood were composed of an infernal liquid, this phrase *search your heart* would mean: consult, follow your diabolic nature, be an impostor, a thief, a murderer, it is the law of your father.

Man is not born wicked; he becomes wicked, as he falls ill. Doctors come along and say: 'You were born ill.' It is quite certain that these doctors, whatever they say and do, will not cure him if his sickness is inherent in his nature; and these thinkers are very ill themselves.

Collect all the children of the universe, and you will see in them only innocence, gentleness and fear. If they were born wicked, evil-doing, cruel, they would show some sign of it, just as small serpents try to bite and little tigers to claw. But nature, not having given more offensive arms to men than to pigeons and rabbits, could not give them an instinct of destruction.

So man is not born evil. Then why are some of them infected by this plague of wickedness? It is because their leaders, being infected by the disease, communicate it to the rest of mankind, just as a woman attacked by the malady brought back from America by Columbus spread this poison from one end of Europe to the other. The first ambitious man corrupted the earth.

You are going to say that this first monster brought out the germ of pride, rapine, fraud, cruelty that is in all men. I admit, generally speaking, that most of our brothers can acquire these qualities; but does everybody have putrid fever, the stone and the gravel because everybody is exposed to them?

There are whole nations that are not wicked: the Philadelphians, the Banians, have never killed anyone; the Chinese, the peoples of Tongking, Laos, Siam, even Japan, have had no war for more than a hundred years. One of the great crimes that shock human nature is hardly seen once in ten years in the cities of Rome, Venice, Paris, London, Amsterdam, although in these cities cupidity, the mother of all crimes, is extreme.

If men were essentially wicked, if they were all born subject to a being as malevolent as he is unhappy, who inspired them with all his rage to avenge himself for his own suffering, we would see every morning husbands murdered by their wives, and fathers by their children, as we find at daybreak chickens strangled by a weasel who came to suck their blood.

If there are a billion men on earth, it is a lot. That would make about 500 million women who sew, spin, feed their little ones, clean their houses or huts, and gossip a little about their neighbours. I do not see what great harm these innocents do on earth. Out of this number of inhabitants of the globe, there are at least 200 million children, who certainly neither kill nor plunder, and about as many old or sick people who are not able to do so. At most there remain 100 million young people, robust and capable of crime. Of these 100 million, 90 million are regularly occupied in prodigious labour to force the earth to yield them food and clothing: these hardly have time to do wrong.

Among the ten million who remain are included the idle and the gregarious, who only want to enjoy themselves; men of talent, busy with their professions; magistrates, priests, obviously concerned to live pure lives, at least in appearance. So the only really wicked men who remain are a few politic individuals, whether secular or religious, who always want to create trouble, and a few thousand vagabonds who hire out their services to these intriguers. In fact, there are never a million of these ferocious beasts employed at one time; and in this number I include highwaymen. So there is at most on earth, in the stormiest times, one man in a thousand who can be called wicked, and even he is not so all the time.

There is thus infinitely less evil on the earth than is said and believed. No doubt there is still too much. Horrible misfortunes and crimes are seen, but the pleasure of complaining and exaggerating is so great that at the slightest scratch you exclaim that the earth overflows with blood. If you have been cheated all men are perjurers. A melancholic who has suffered an injustice sees the universe covered with the damned, just as a young voluptuary, supping with his lady after the opera, cannot imagine that unfortunates exist.